D1693487

For Térése, Micah, and Miles
For Julianne, Savion, and Daven

Titus
Kaphar

Reginald Dwayne Betts

Redaction

W. W. Norton & Company
Independent publishers since 1923

A journey through words & images meant to trouble;
A poet & a painter, refuse to let them blackhole this process.

Titus Kaphar and Reginald Dwayne Betts

Redaction

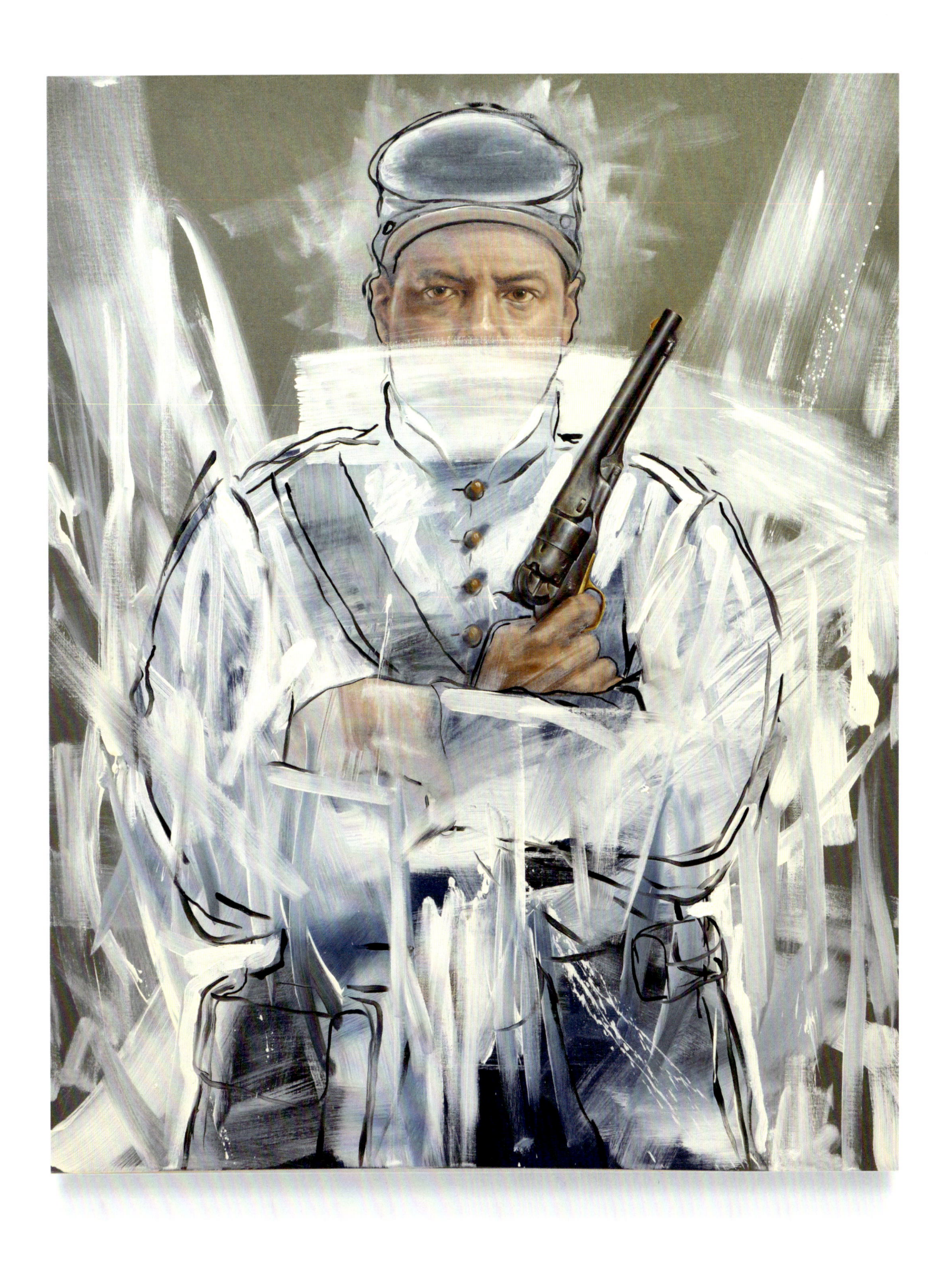

None of the illustrations in this book are intended as a literal representation of any living individual. Further, the illustrations in the *Redaction* sections do not portray any party involved in any of the lawsuits referenced. Rather, these images are meant to convey the universality of the injustices perpetrated by our criminal justice system.

14	Sarah Suzuki **Introduction**		

19	Archive 1	41	**Redaction 1**
85	Archive 2	103	**Redaction 2**
137	Archive 3	151	**Redaction 3**

190	Forest Young and Jeremy Mickel **Redaction Typeface: A Multiplicity of Typographic, Legal, and Human Histories**
194	List of Works
195	Acknowledgments
196	Credits

Exhibition view: *Pleading Freedom: An Exhibition by Titus Kaphar and Reginald Dwayne Betts*, NXTHVN, New Haven, 2020

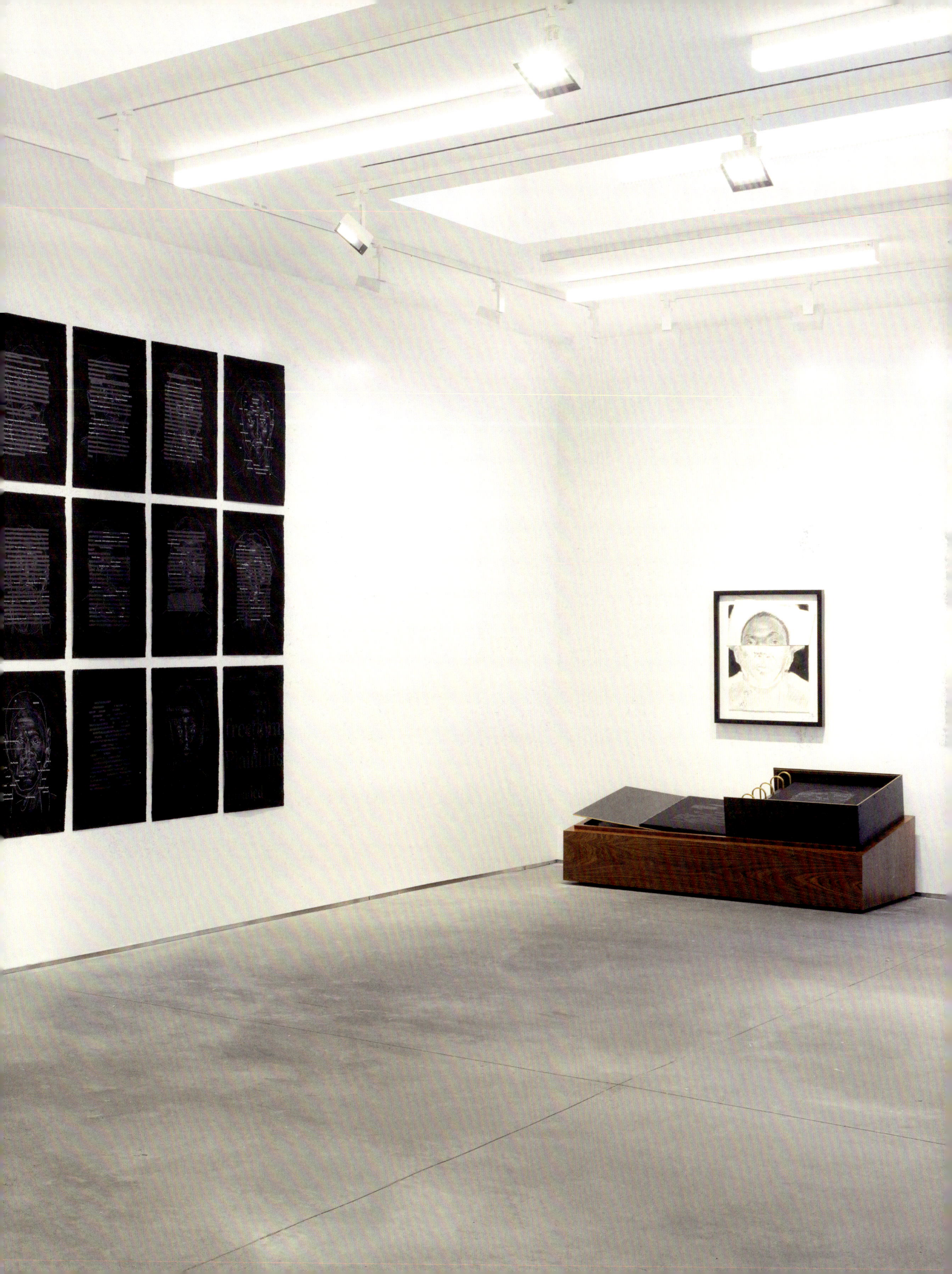

Exhibition view: *Redaction: A Project by Titus Kaphar and Reginald Dwayne Betts*, MoMA PS1, New York, 2019

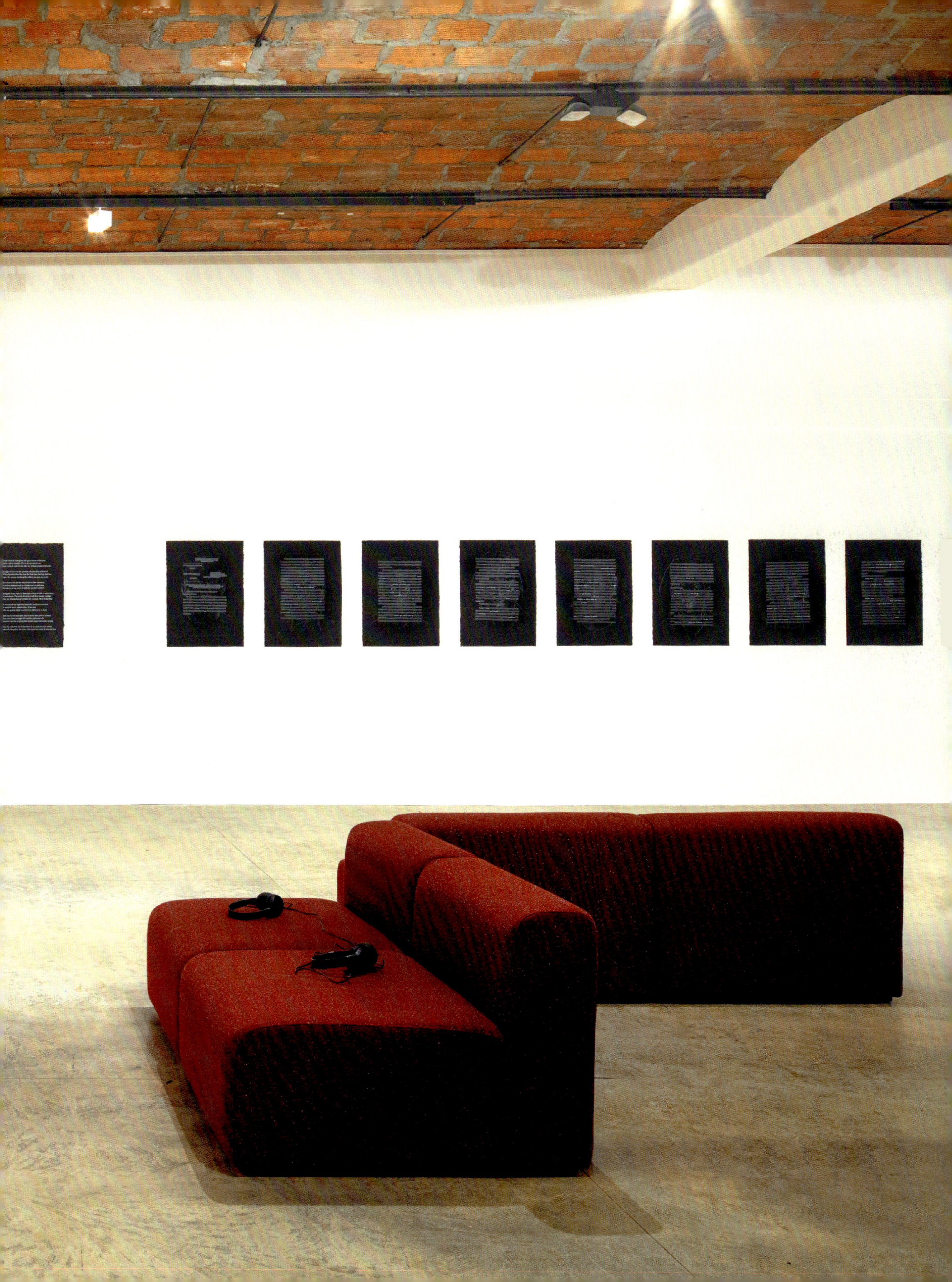

Sarah Suzuki
Introduction

In 2018, an old friend, the visual artist and filmmaker Titus Kaphar, introduced me to a new one, the poet, memoirist, and attorney Reginald Dwayne Betts, over coffee at the Museum of Modern Art. In that first conversation together, we touched on art and poetry and work and life, and then they told me about a collaborative project on which they had begun work: a print portfolio, with images by Kaphar and poems by Betts, that would explore the criminal justice system's multifarious failings, a central focus for both artists in their work and their lives, and the subject of intense public discussion and debate.

The project, *Redaction*, sought to dive deeply into a specific problem: the exploitative concept of money bail, the practice of state and federal court systems by which those arrested, but unable to afford bail, remain incarcerated even though they have been neither tried nor convicted.

A visit to the Lower East Side Printshop, where the project was underway, signaled the variety and breadth of possibilities at play: papers in different colors and textures, made from pulped textiles and other materials; inks translucent and opaque, metallic and matte; text and image, text overlaid on image, image overlaid on text; permutations and variations on different combinations of printing plates. It also showed two blazing talents at the height of their respective powers.

In his verse, Betts impactfully employs the tactic of redaction, blanking out words and phrases from pre-existing texts to craft poetry. He uses, as source material for these poems, lawsuits the Civil Rights Corps (CRC) filed on behalf of people arguing that their constitutional rights were violated when they were forced to remain incarcerated because they could not pay bail or traffic tickets or court fees. In the poet's hands, the technique is inverted: rather than redaction concealing the most sensitive information, here it reveals the essence of the personal stories buried within the documents. With captivating cadence and precision syncopation, Betts unearths humanity, frustration, and passion from unfeeling, pseudo-neutral legalese.

In his extraordinary etchings, Kaphar creates portraits of men, women, and children that manifest their subjects' precarity. Subverting the traditional choice of printing black ink on white paper, Kaphar instead prints on black paper, his white lines evasive, evanescent wisps that threaten to slip our visual grasp and disappear, just as their subjects might disappear into a system rigged against them. Images are superimposed but off-register, shimmering, challenging our eyes to bring them into focus and actually see them.

As the voices of the persecuted and the persecutors that make these bail decisions emerge from Betts's verse, they transform Kaphar's images from potentially anonymous depictions to those of familiars, as we recall faces of friends and family and begin to think of them in context of these stories that become familiar — the dockworker from San Francisco, the mother with unpaid parking tickets. The collaborative alchemy of Kaphar and Betts asks us to see, to look, to read, to listen closely.

In the spring of 2019, a suite of 30 pages from *Redaction* were shared with the public for the first time in an exhibition at MoMA PS1 in New York. The project spoke urgently to the moment, and sought to create a platform for a multiplicity of conversations — about art, poetry, and practical legal questions — that had the potential to offer support, influence outcomes, and reflect current conversations around the issue of criminal justice reform. *Redaction* resonated with audiences on multivalent levels: the images compelled, the poetry was magnetic, and the questions framed were urgent and timely, and addressed themselves to communities that too rarely see themselves reflected back from the walls of the museum.

And while *Redaction* exists with urgency in the present, invites contemplation and discussion, and will surely be an artistic landmark of our time, it also marks a new entry in a storied history within modern art, that of illustrated books or *livres d'artistes*. This book form, comprising text and image conceived as a unified conceptual whole, was reclaimed by artists at the end of the nineteenth century and has evolved and been reconceptualized many times since then. While formally *livres d'artistes* range from modest, self-published *samizdat* of the Russian avant garde, to the luxuriously produced volumes of French publishing impresario Ambroise Vollard, the best *livres d'artistes* are rich terrain for formal and literary invention. They also require myriad decisions, large and small, that build toward a vision of a book-object as a holistic totality.

In his *Calligrammes* of 1918, Guillaume Apollinaire explored how typeface and the spatial arrangement of words on a page create meaning as powerfully as the words themselves do. For their project, Kaphar and Betts collaborated on a new, open-source font with designers Jeremy Mickel and Forest Young. Available for free public download, the Redaction font abstracts and distorts familiar serifed fonts like Century Schoolbook, standard for legal documents in the United States, with letterforms that have been themselves redacted in key places. With this, the artists create an opportunity for *Redaction* to seed itself into the legal system as a kind of active, ongoing, circulating protest.

And while traditionally many *livres d'artistes* have focused on subjects of pleasure — think fables, mythologies, bestiaries, and poetry — there are antecedents that confront difficult subjects, and ask us to think deeply and critically about issues. Francisco de Goya's *Disasters of War*, a landmark series of 82 etchings, depicted the gruesome human cost of the Peninsular War accompanied by short, poetic captions of the artist's own devising. *Voina*, a 1916 collaboration between artist Olga Rozanova and her husband, poet Aleksei Kruchenykh, drew on newspaper accounts of horrific events of World War I with pages in which she carved his text and her images seamlessly onto linoleum blocks for printing.

Redaction is the twenty-first century continuation of this history of literary and artistic projects that transcend time, and become tools for understanding the past from the vantage of the present. In a process of true collaboration, in which word and image each hold space, yet do more together, amplifying each other. But it is simultaneously of our moment, an urgent project offered by artistic and literary leaders to show us a path forward. Together, Betts's verse and Kaphar's printed portraits blend the voices of poet and artist with those of the plaintiffs and prosecutors, reclaiming these lost narratives and drawing attention to some of the many individuals whose lives have been impacted by mass incarceration in a landmark *livre d'artiste* for the twenty-first century.

Sarah Suzuki is Associate Director at the Museum of Modern Art (MoMA), New York.

Archive 1

Titus Kaphar and Reginald Dwayne Betts

& Crispus Attucks's two dead eyes,
Vacant as a confederate soldier's,
Empty as some stories of tomorrow
& tomorrow & tomorrow: & every
Tomorrow somehow its own
Chronicle, each spiel more lovely
& devastating than the last & tell me
The story of the eyes of some dead man
Refusing to be a witness & Oh Lord
This democracy, this becoming,
These amendments that metamorph
To Kafka's pet, some euphemism
For longing, for firearms, for death,
For loss, for this suffering: three-fifths
The whole person, three-fifths & Indians,
May be excluded, from this Union,
Respective of numbers, apportioned;
All three-fifths, Indians, three-fifths
Not free persons, Indians, not free —
Bound to service & Crispus whose
Body bled for this democracy becomes
A jeopardy question & Oh Lord
This democracy — this woolgathering
Confession: not Indian, but Mohegan,
Mojave, *Manhattan is a Lenape
Word*; not three-fifths, an abundance,
A history & Crispus caught a bullet
With his patriotism, his dead body
counted first, as if being counted
Is a prerequisite to freedom for this
America & its graveyards of naming.

During my second semester at Yale Law School, I carried around the letters of a dead man. I began to think of them as small pieces of the prison cells that once held him. The letters were from Glenn McGinnis—executed on January 25, 2000, for the murder of Leta Wilkerson. & all I know of her is the bullet from McGinnis that killed her. Every memory of a murder burying so many. A tempest, all of it. & the letters conveyed every emotion but fear. Mostly. In time the one-sided correspondence came to symbolize my own terror: that prison would be the shadow I carried until my death.

That semester I took Professor Stephen Bright's capital punishment course. Before then, my knowledge of death row consisted of McGinnis's letters & a story from my time at Sussex 1 State Prison. From the pull-up bar, I couldn't help but hear a young man, new to the compound, talking to a friend locked in a cell that faced the yard. The window in the cell was no wider than the palm of a hand, no longer than the length of a tall man's arm. I watched them trying to communicate. They weren't talking as much as yelling & reading each other's lips. The new guy asked his friend when he was getting out. The response: *I'm on death row*.

For men on death row, leaving a cell is not a move toward freedom but one toward death.

McGinnis committed murder at 17. Ellis Unit One at the Texas State Penitentiary became his home. His letters became a way to escape the cell that held him. These letters speak to the desperation that comes with being haunted by the specter of death. Many begin with poems: "I don't dare start thinking in the morning. / I don't dare start thinking in the morning." Another begins: "My luck is short like dust." Neither poems nor the letters dwell on the small details of a death sentence: the hours in a cell thinking of ways to save yourself, the fear of friends' executions, the waiting for word from the governor, waiting for the miracle that rarely comes.

Nearly everything about a prison can be hidden in a letter. McGinnis's letters bury his sadness. But sometimes it comes through. "Mr. K told me that my appeals has been exhausted & he has no hope of me getting off death row." The letters in my bag reminded me, again, how legal theories can hasten death.

Prisons are places where possibility goes to die. But the lives men live & the letters—the letters they write push against that. I cannot disconnect the cell from the letter. Back then we called letters *kites*, as if ambition & hope alone could give a word wings. & it was true—words could escape the darkness of the cell. The paper, the envelopes, the very ink used to scratch those words into existence carries with it the funk of prison & the memory of a jail cell. McGinnis's letters collapsed the inexorable distance between me & prison. Relics from all cells that he had served time in, his letters allow me to think of the prison's architecture as defined by the words that escape. & still the details haunt. In the letter where McGinnis talks about his appeals being exhausted, he writes, "I apologize for not being able to write you a more gracious letter."

Prison snuffs out light. This is what I know: from a cell you begin writing about your troubles & realize the burden of your words. & so you hold back. McGinnis's letters came to me nearly a decade after they were written, when he was already dead. They made me see how much I'd held back; all the pain & anguish. His letters came before I decided to go to law school, before I could possibly understand their legal implications—what it means to be sentenced to die for a crime you committed as a teenager.

On the last day of class, Professor Bright played a video of Steve Earle's "Ellis Unit One." Earle had been a correctional officer in the Texas State Prison before becoming a country singer. McGinnis's letters were in my backpack. In the same way that men scratch their names, their lives, on cell walls to remind people that they were there, he etched part of his life in letters. In 2005, the Supreme Court ruled in *Roper v. Simmons* that executing people for crimes committed before they turned 18 violates the Eighth Amendment's prohibition against cruel & unusual punishment. If McGinnis had been on death row in just about any other state in the country, his appeals would have taken a few years longer & he would have lived to see the Supreme Court decision. Today only his letters are left—his letters & memories.

FELON

POEMS

REGINALD DWAYNE BETTS

Titus Kaphar and Reginald Dwayne Betts

A woman disappears behind the face
Of a man. Negro child, girl child, Black child

What is the language for forgotten? Hidden
Behind a veil of declared independence.

Not a single signature would have confessed
Her name in public. The lesson of owning

Begins with erasure. Who confuses a woman
For property. (Many men, many many many

Many men.) Not someone else, mister & master.
Not mistress — But eclipse. Blacker

Than cotton falling into the shade of a sack longer
Than her frail body. How do you say child

In the language of a whip post?
Behind him, the sound of a woman effaced.

The office of expunction:
Man & ownership & the collateral of it all, a body

Sprawled against its own vanquishing.
Always half the tale. What wasn't lost

In the chronicle? Hosannas. All men created
With a backdrop of a woman forced

Into this awkward submission? Lascivious becomes
Something mutual. Negro girl slave girl slave girl

As lover black girl as lover black woman as lover
Permission as lost continent.

The conundrum is unmasked by a knife
Against the canvas. Behind the man

A woman shackled to what? The ghost rib?

Whatever about expectations,
On a Monday the small birds sing
The same & again I do not call my
Father. There is something about these
Stories we don't tell. My father told me
Success is a synonym for random or
Coincidence or, as he called it, his favorite
Word: happenstance. He had never called
Me happenstance but there is something
Of that to this & so on one of those
Happenstance Mondays I was in my garden
Hoping to make more than my regret grow.
Learning to weed is more proxy of science
Than science, & more happenstance than
Skill. But I'd learned to notice what was new,
& then decide if the new was beauty. I've
Always wanted to be called lovely &
Held with the tenderness of a man sliding
A tire off a car on bricks at midnight.
Whatever about being held. On that Monday,
I noticed the vines of a tomato & thought
Of my father. Did I mention he gardens?
All of my stories are about this man. Once
He told me about volunteer tomatoes,
Said they only come to those who'll honor
The gift of fruit unasked for. I took off my
Gloves before tenderly touching the green
Globes. Such a certain kind of surprise,
A wonder, something left over by a visitor
I might not have wanted, some squirrel or
Bird or g–d. & though the green thing in my
Hand was not rightly yet a tomato, I sank
My teeth into its not yet tender flesh.

Redaction

Titus Kaphar and Reginald Dwayne Betts

Sitting still, on a street with a name
I cannot recall, is a Coupe Deville.
I always wanted to sing, seduce
A crowd with the terrible in my voice,
& mornings, driving by this song
Of my past, often I slow as if to see
Is to climb behind the wheel & return
To the moment that could have
Changed it all. I sweated that ride
Like I worried over finding my falsetto,
Even after Amaud let me know *to reach
those notes—a man essentially cuts
his own throat*. Something about desire
Frightens me. I started to love that canary
Spaceship & then discovered *de ville*
Is a French word for town hall:
Maybe some don't need an audience.
I didn't expect to land here, where
I tell you there is no city for me
To claim, admit I've learned to belong
In what meaning comes from this
Cadillac that never moves, but reminds
Me of times when all my baggage
Was expectation. A lover once showed
Me how everyone deserves to expect
Tenderness. & I drive by that version
Of my yesterdays & know that there is
Always something to cherish so much
It makes you sigh, as some longing might.

Fugitive Slave Act of 1793

fugitives   **persons escaping**

a fugitive
person
fled
any

the person   fled
person   fled
the
prisoner   the
fugitive

the fugitive
empowered   he
or she   fled   the
fugitive   the person
not   imprisoned not

held
the person
fugitive
Judge   United States,
the State   county, city, or town
shall be made
oral testimony
that the person
fled

the fugitive
fled.
knowingly and willingly
such fugitive
such fugitive
given   harbor
a fugitive
recovered
by   saving
his   account of   injuries

Approved [signed into law by President George Washington], February 12, 1793.

Titus Kaphar and Reginald Dwayne Betts

Redaction

Titus Kaphar and Reginald Dwayne Betts

34

A group of almost anything
Has a name: crows are a murder,
& flamingoes a flamboyance.
Most of the others I don't know.
A group of empty shot glasses
Is called a disaster; of empty
Rooms, a yesterday; a collection
Of tomorrows, even if dreamed,
If desired, craved for like some
Small child wanting one more story
At bedtime, is called hope. Too
Many nights when all I had was hope.
No collective noun exists to hold
All the people you love. If we name
It at all wouldn't it be abundance?
I have an abundance of loves
& even when I am lonely, especially
Then, they show up. It rains outside,
& inside everyone I love sleeps.
There is no word for listening
To them breathe, but if there were,
It would be the antithesis of murder.
Crows always remember a face,
Is what I read once, & can recall it as if
A part of a dream, & so I've always
Thought a house full of loves
Is a dreaming, & what better word
For listening to all your loves breathe
At night than a dreaming? What more
Could any of us ask of the dusk?

If I return, it'll start with a pistol,
The dark a mask that never hides
Enough. I'll pour the last of my drink
Down so fast, I'll choke & cough.
If I return, the past that I pretend
Defines me — won't explain the old
Familiar feeling of cuffs that capture
My hand's ambition & escort
Me past the Mason Dixon.
I'll remind myself that *the first time
I traveled south was to go to prison*.
My legacy will be in my head,
Rattling around in a four-door sedan
With fucked up suspension. I'll be
Headed back to where time buries
The times of men. My return will
Carry me through an entire state
Of cities named after prisons.
& my yesterdays will become
The water that drowns. If I return,
My sons may forget my name: inmate,
Convict, prisoner, jailbird, felon —
Will all fail. & there will be
No word for this thing I've become.

Titus Kaphar and Reginald Dwayne Betts

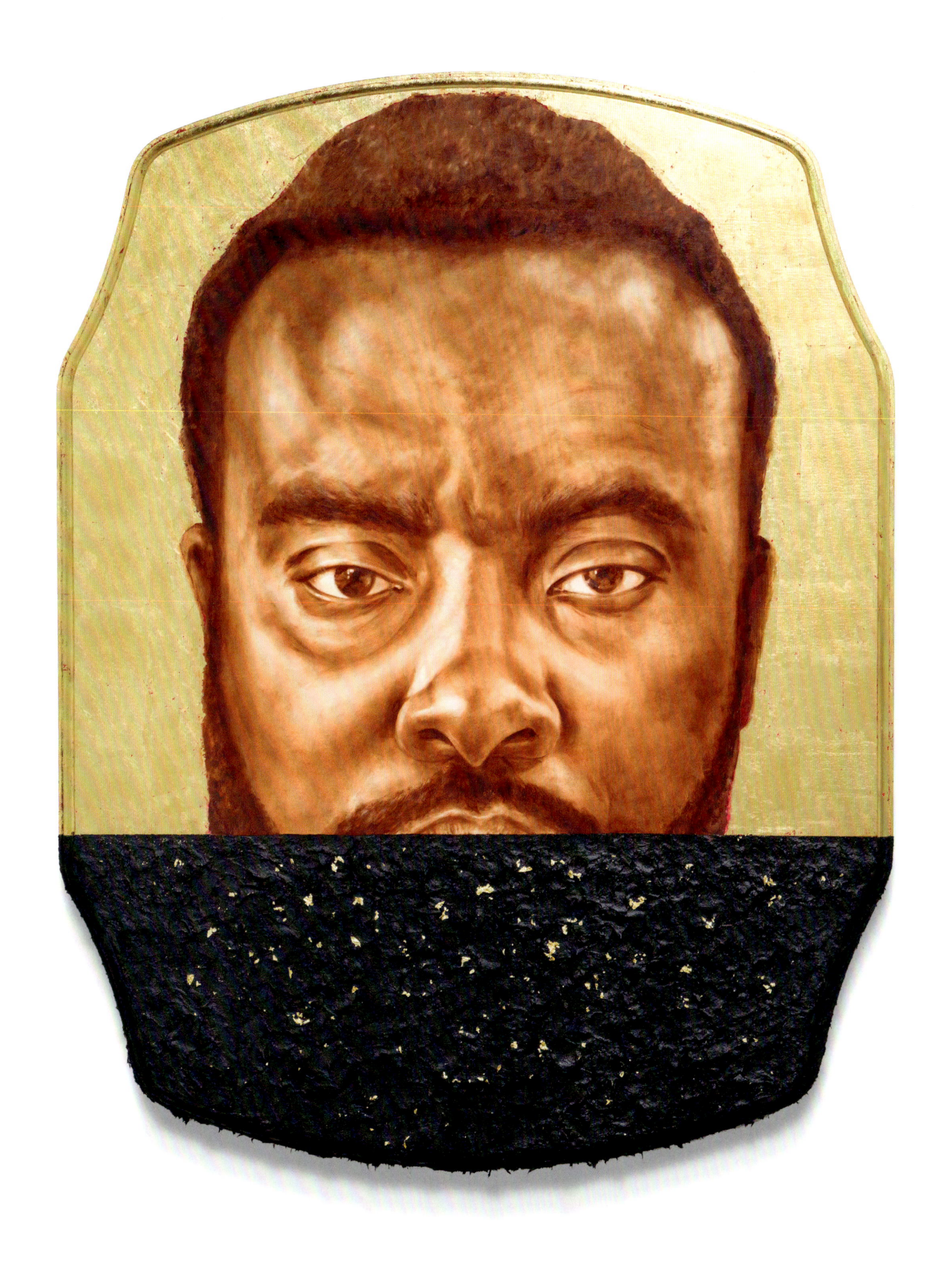

Redaction

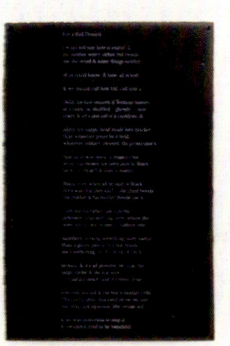

Exhibition view: *Pleading Freedom: An Exhibition by Titus Kaphar and Reginald Dwayne Betts*, NXTHVN, New Haven, 2020

committed
legislature
pleaded
Plaintiffs.
freedom
Habeas
Corpus
freedom
Plaintiffs
pleaded

Redaction 1

Titus Kaphar and Reginald Dwayne Betts,
Redaction portfolio, 2019

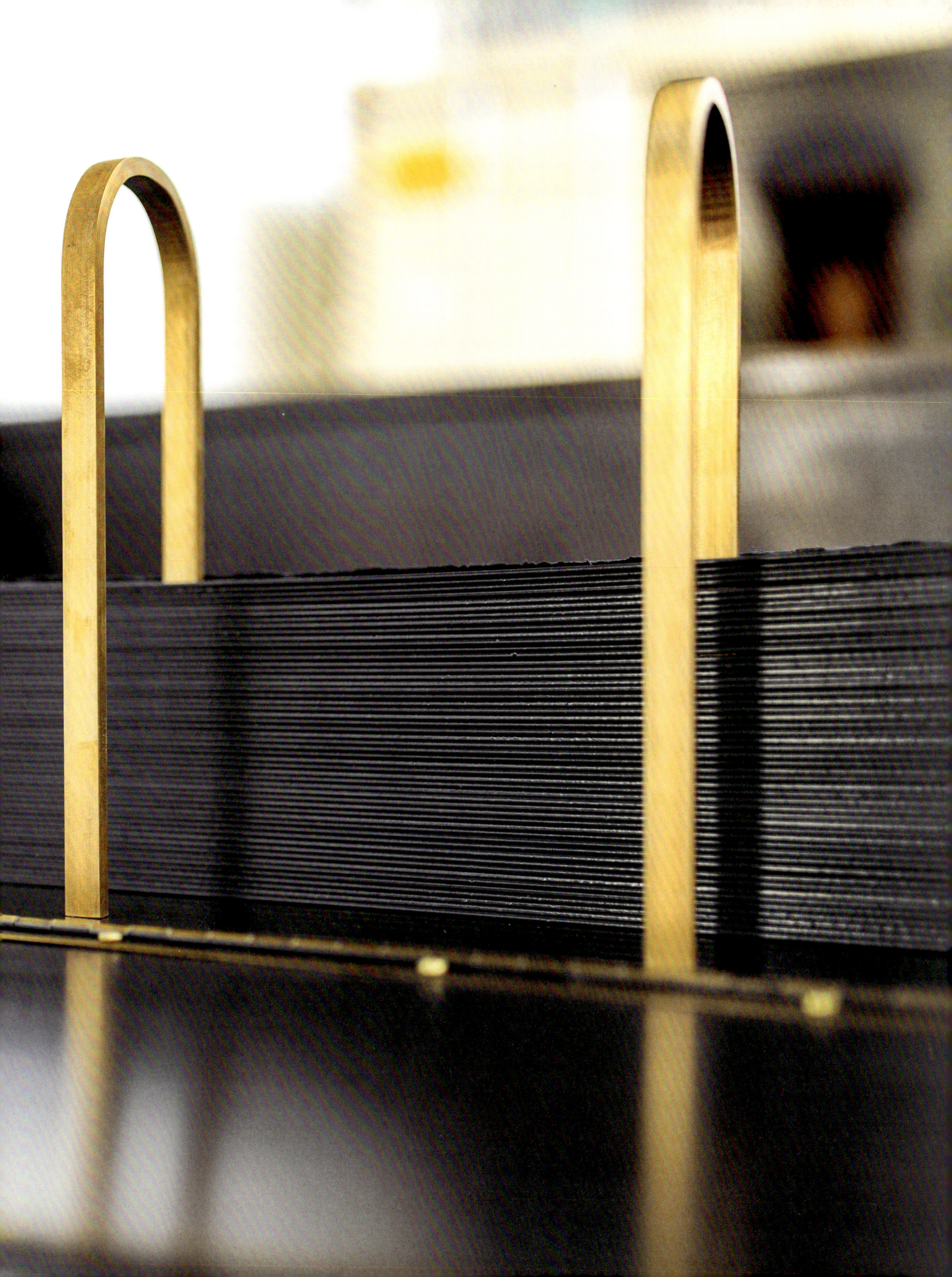

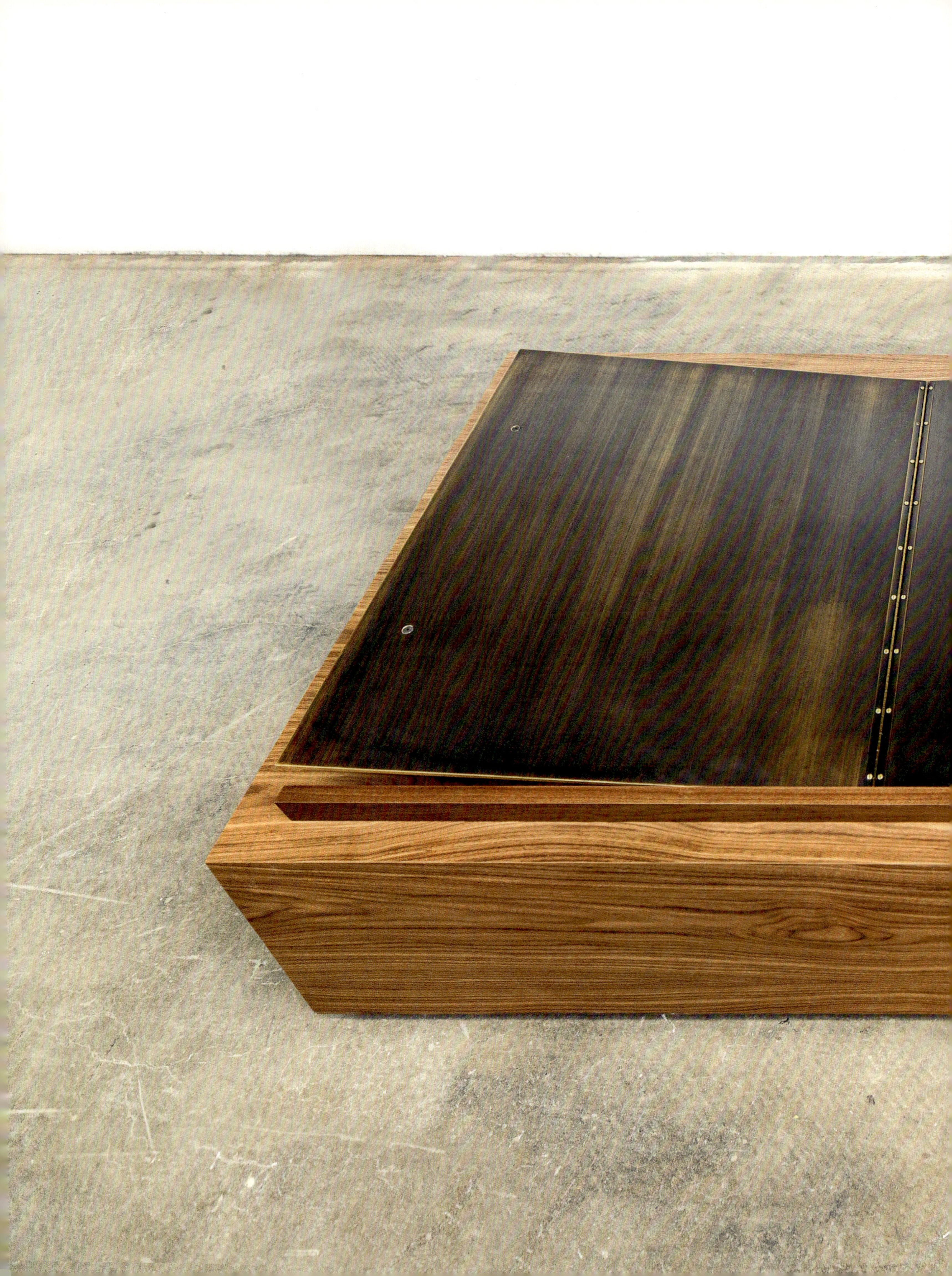

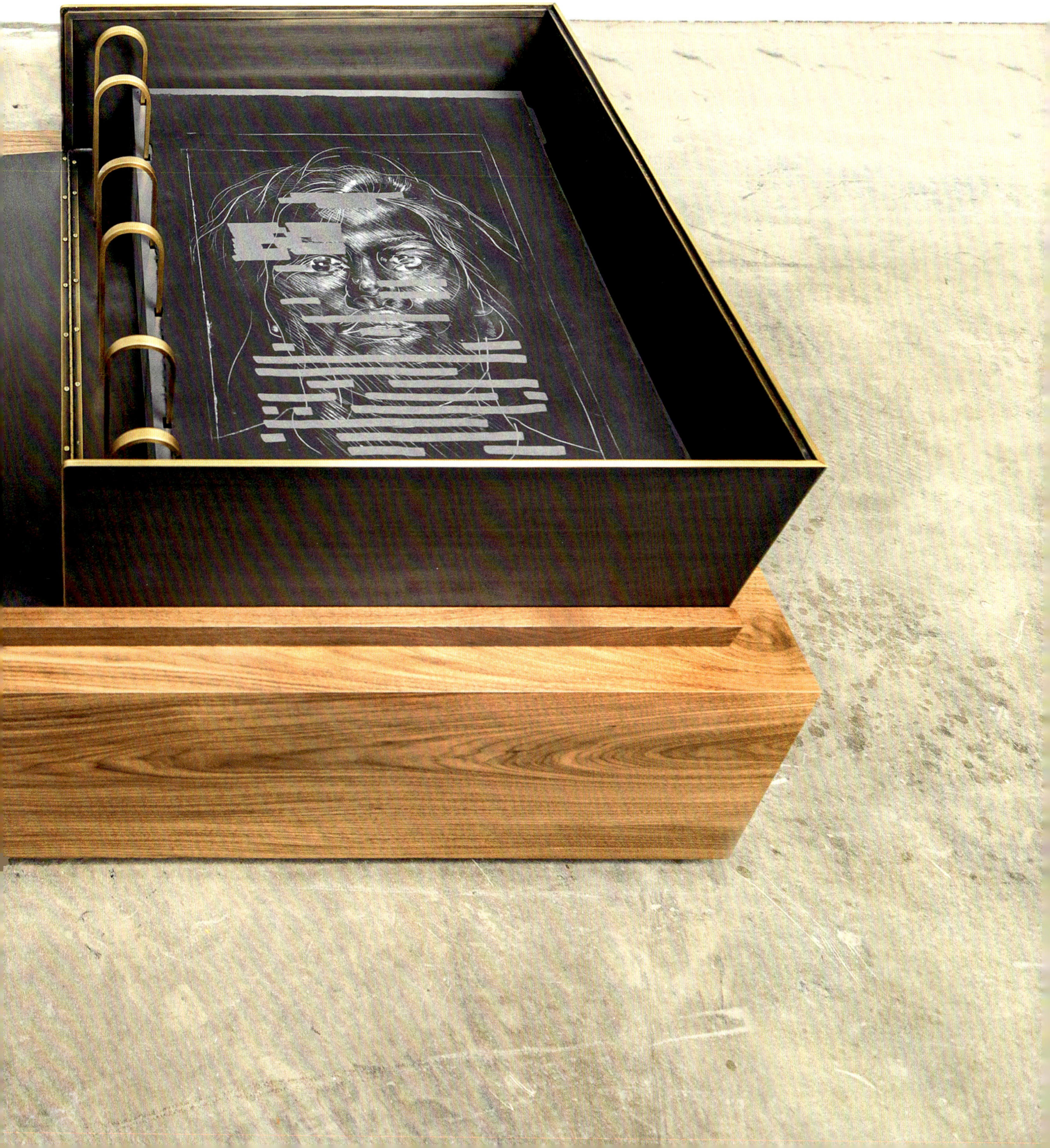

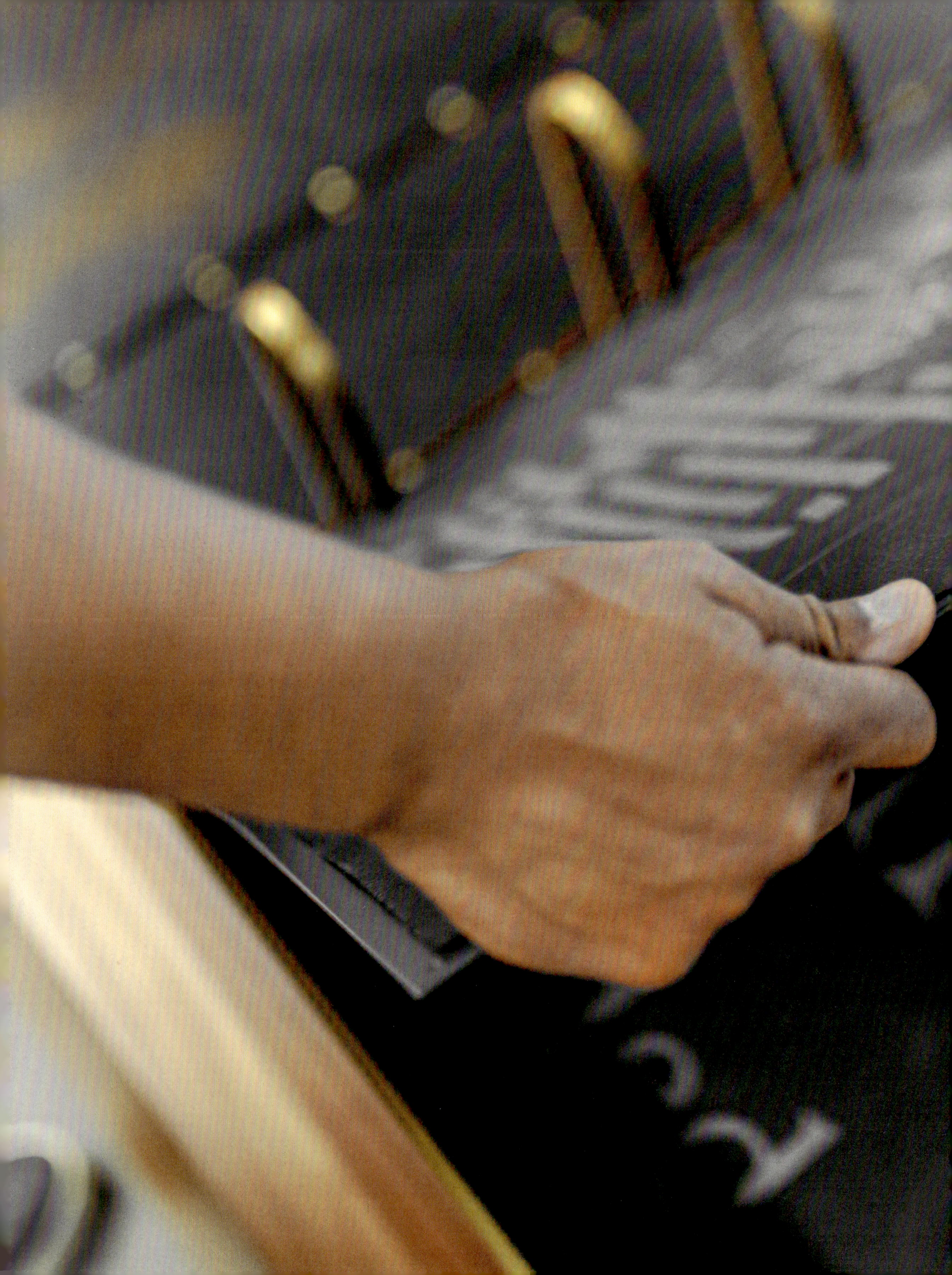

dom
tif

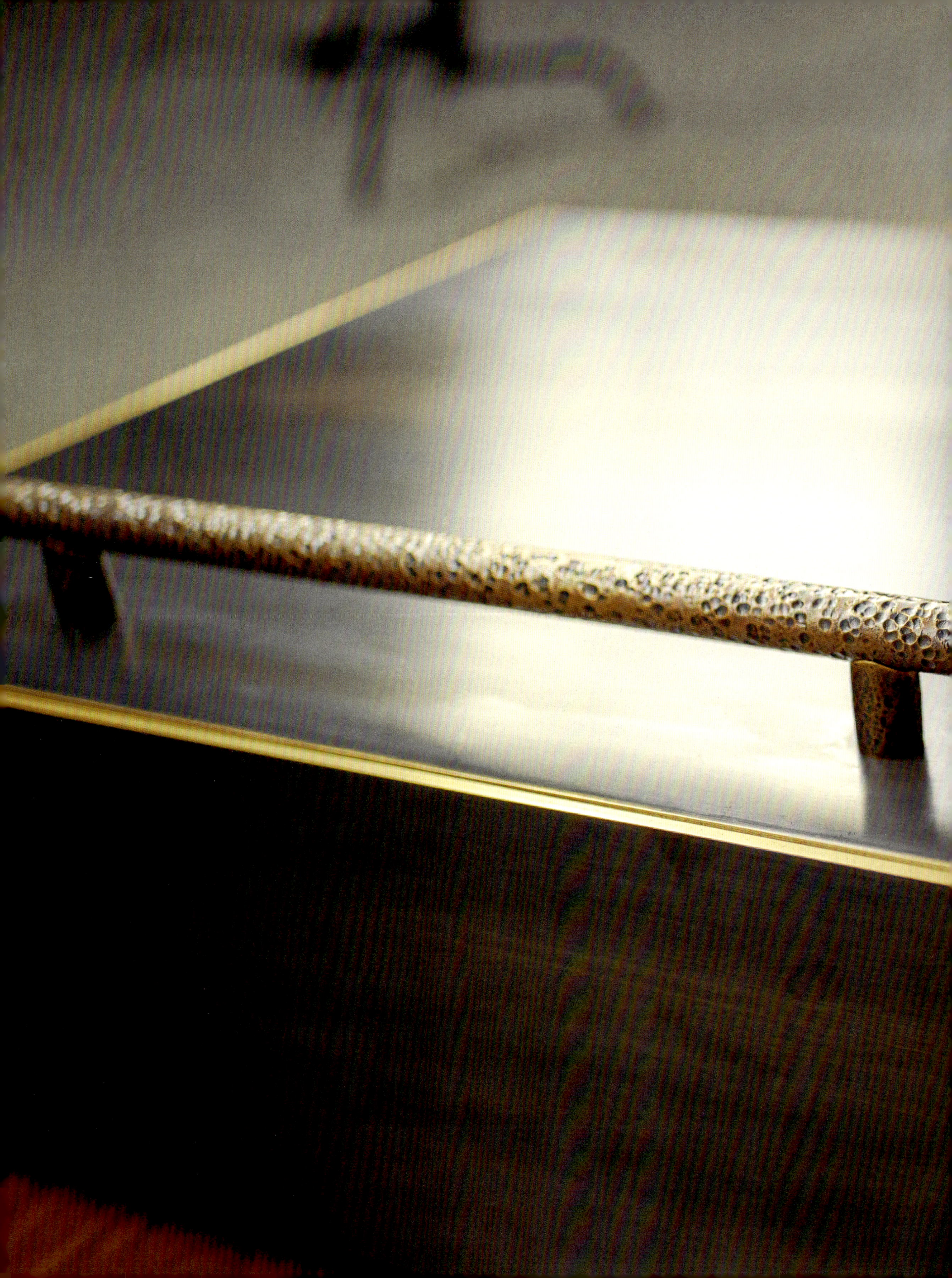

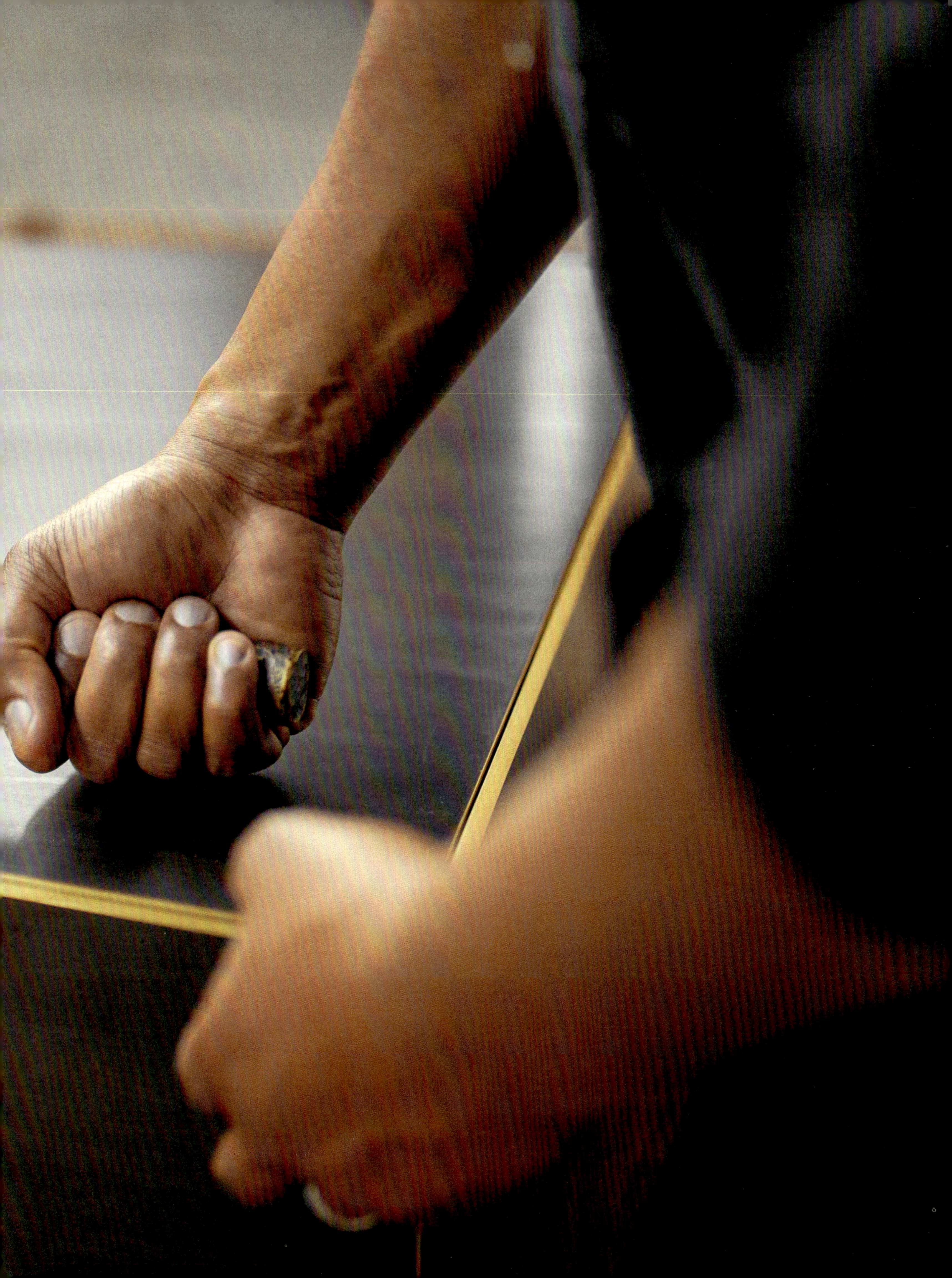

Titus Kaphar and Reginald Dwayne Betts

REDACTION

Redaction, October 2022

This publication, in its physical form and its circulation,
constitutes the third exhibition of this work.

Cloth casebound smyth-sewn softcover

9 ½ × 12 × ¾ in.

Contains 50 works printed offset on Fedrigoni Sirio Color Black
with white and metallic Pantone inks

Special edition volume contains an enclosed sheet of handmade paper
sourced from two materials: (1) t-shirts and towels made by men serving time
in prison, working for pennies on the dollar & (2) clothing worn by
friends of Dwayne serving time in Virginia prisons. These men all know him
as Shahid & remember when he called those cells home.

Paper handmade by Master Printer & Papermaker Ruth Lingen

※

Printed by Die Keure, Bruges, Belgium

Based on a previous edition printed by Lower East Side Printshop, NYC
Master Printer Erik Hougen

Redaction font designed by Jeremy Mickel of MCKL Studios
with creative direction by Forest Young and
collaborators Titus Kaphar and Reginald Dwayne Betts

The inaugural exhibition of this work was at MoMA PS1,
March 2019, curated by Sarah Suzuki.

A second exhibition of this work was shown as part of *Pleading Freedom*
at NXTHVN, August–September, 2020.

IN THE MIDDLE OF ALABAMA
_____

v

THE CITY OF MONTGOMERY

      The Plaintiffs   impoverished   jailed by the City   unable to pay traffic tickets   pay   or sit   jail $50 per day   Plaintiffs   unable to pay   each sent to jail

      told they could   work off debts $25 per day   cleaning the   City   scrubbing feces and blood from jail floors

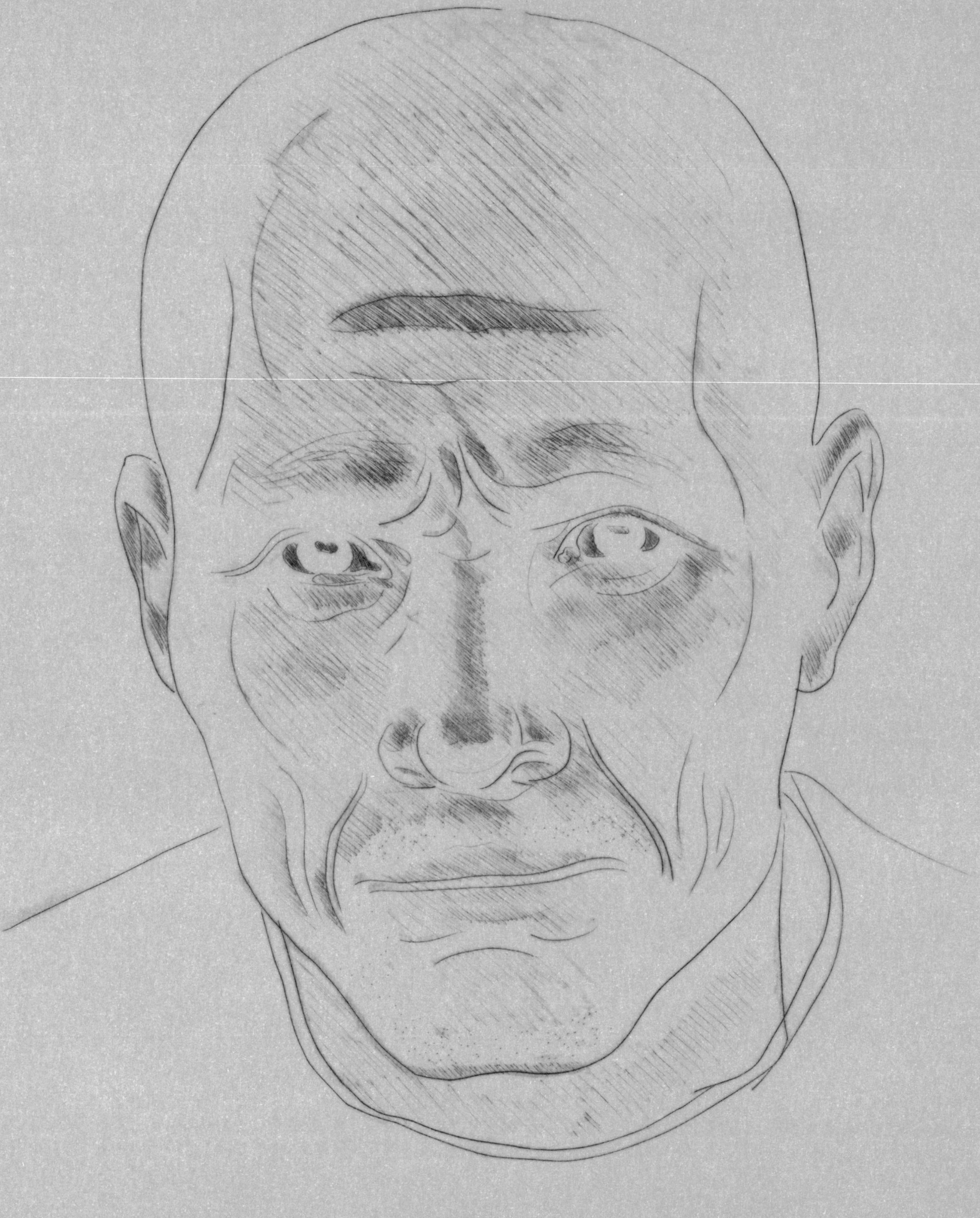

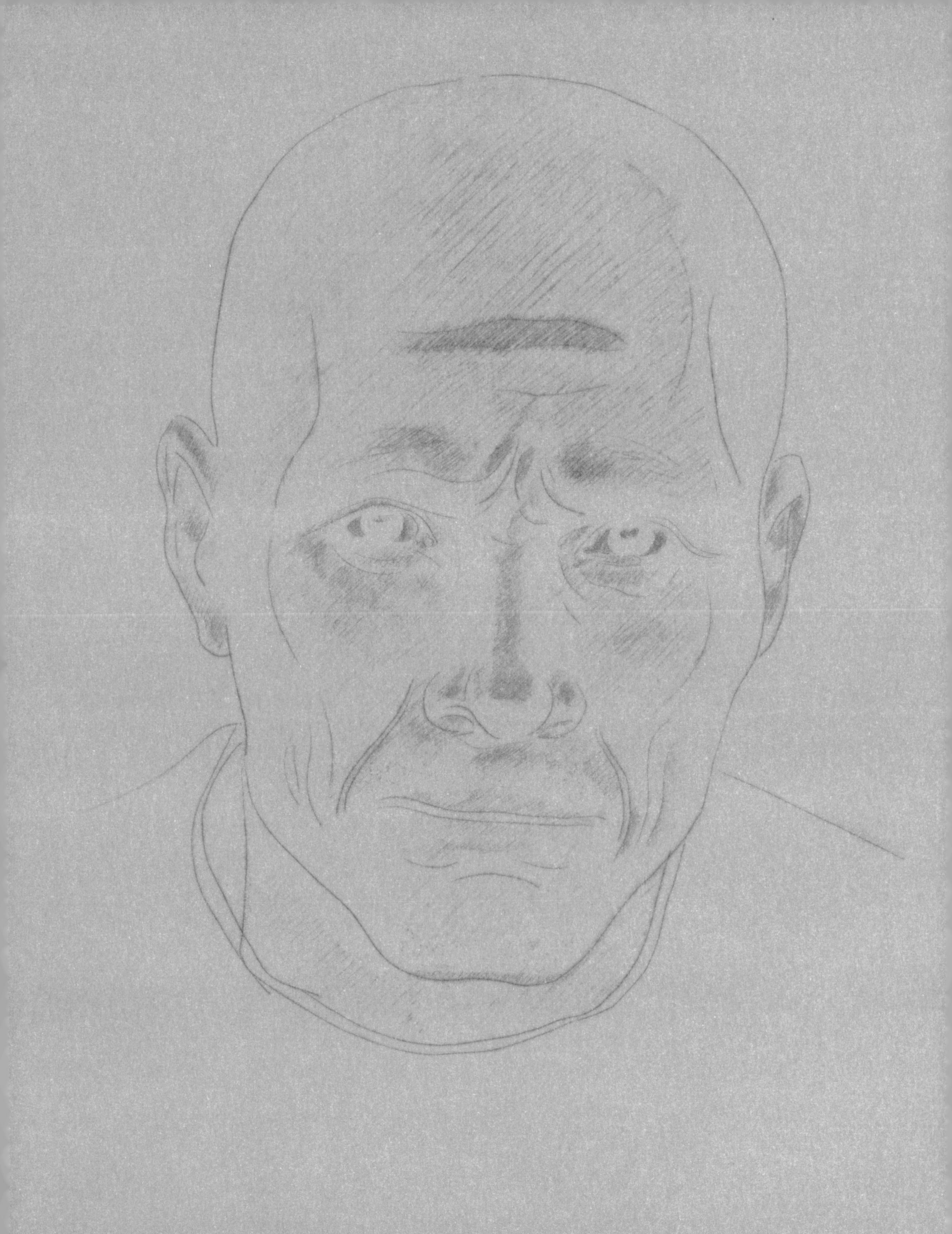

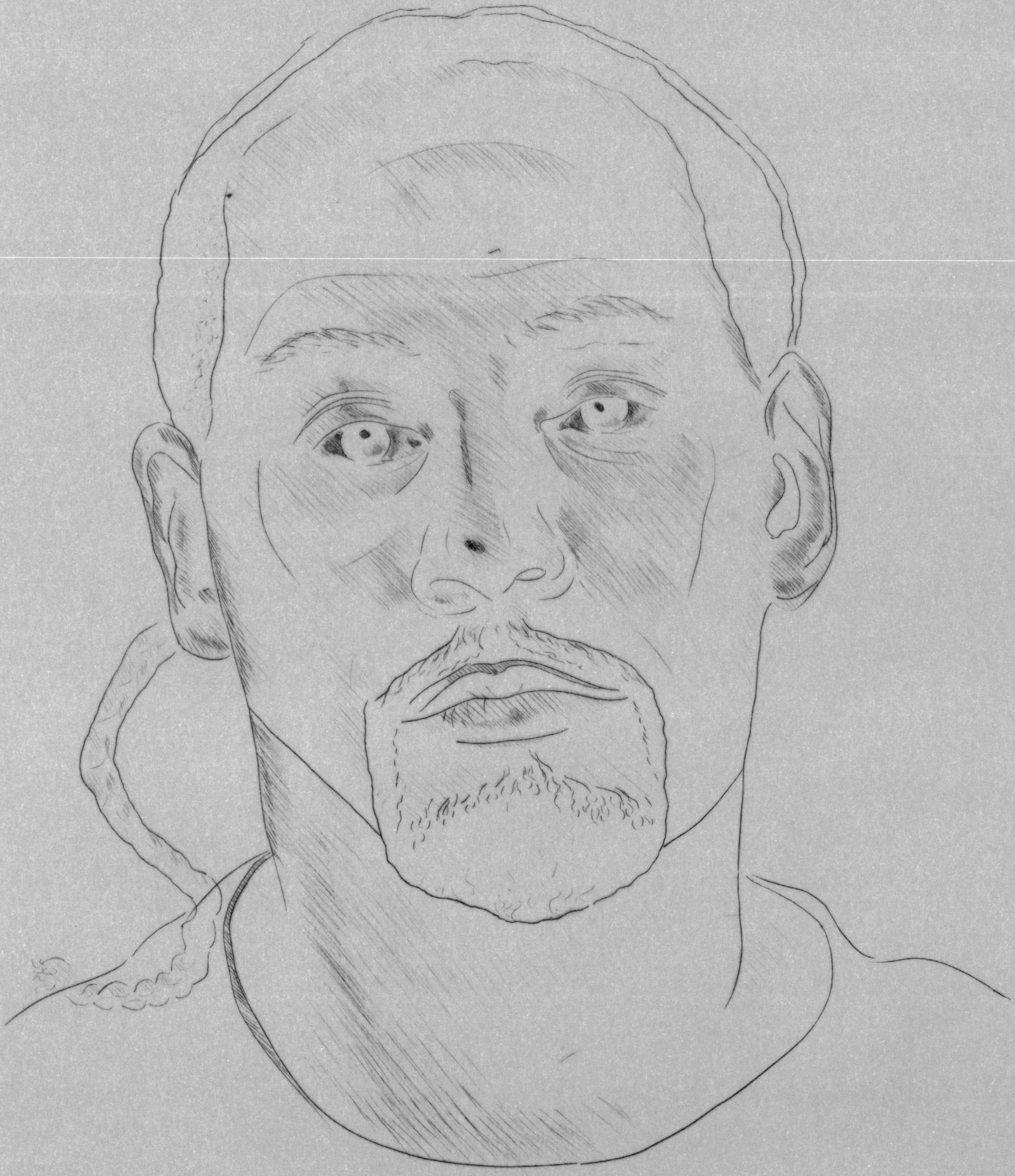

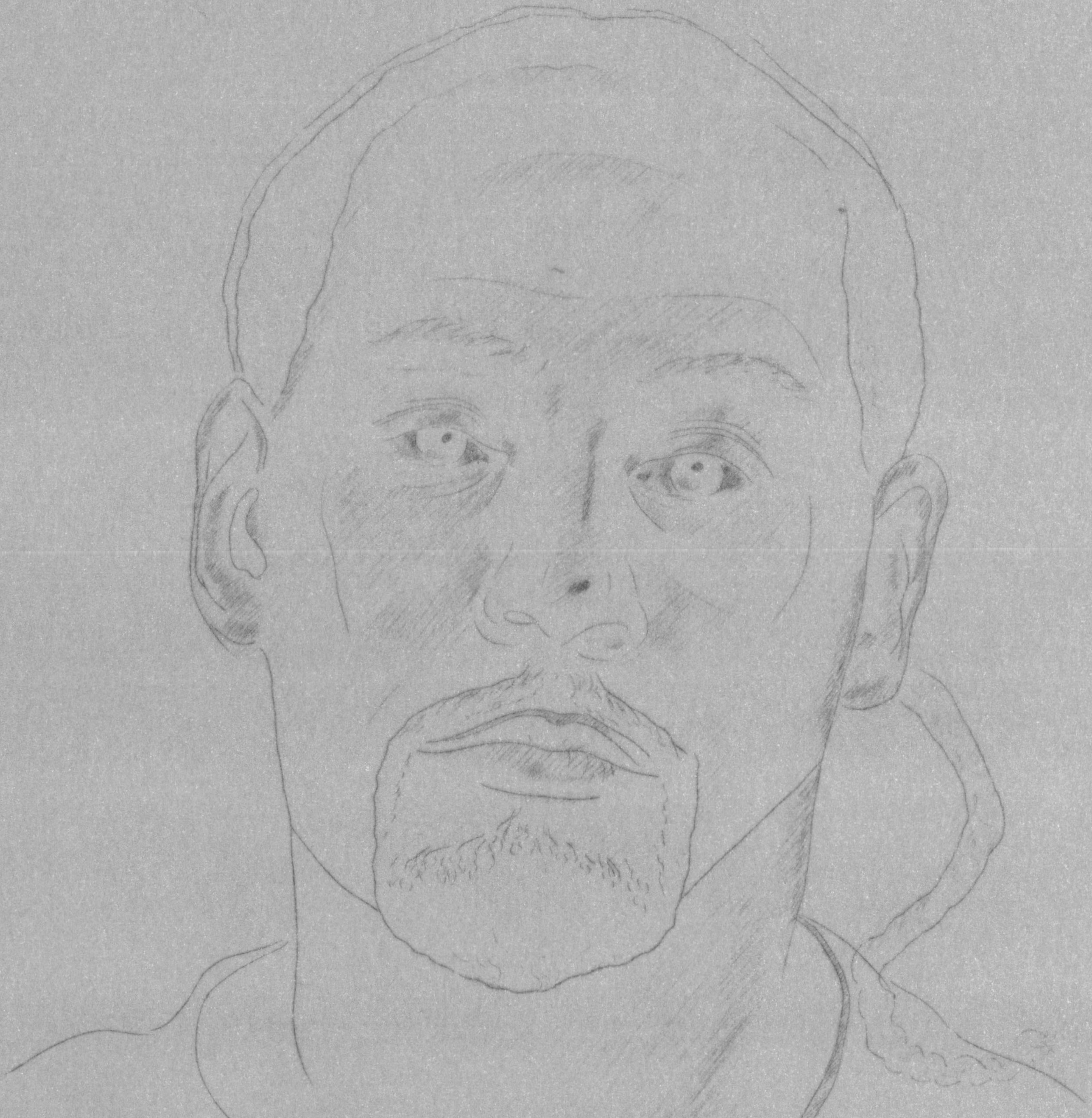

IN THE MIDDLE OF ALABAMA

v.

THE CITY OF MONTGOMERY

The Plaintiffs impoverished jailed by the City unable to pay traffic tickets pay or sit jail $50 per day Plaintiffs unable to pay each sent to jail told they could work off debts $25 per day cleaning the City scrubbing feces and blood from jail floors

The treatment reveals the City against its poorest

jailing people if they poor

Plaintiffs seek
fundamental rights they suffered the
City's unlawful

It is the policy ▓▓▓ of the City ▓▓▓ to jail people
▓▓▓▓▓▓▓▓▓▓▓▓▓▓▓▓▓▓▓▓▓▓▓▓▓▓▓▓▓▓▓▓
▓▓▓▓▓▓▓▓▓▓▓▓▓▓▓▓▓▓▓▓▓▓▓▓▓▓▓▓▓▓▓▓
▓▓▓▓▓▓▓▓▓▓▓▓▓▓▓▓▓▓▓▓▓▓▓▓▓▓▓▓▓▓▓▓
It is the policy ▓▓▓ of the City to jail ▓▓▓ people ▓
▓▓▓▓▓▓▓▓▓▓▓▓▓▓▓▓▓▓▓▓▓▓▓▓▓▓▓▓▓▓▓▓
▓▓▓▓▓▓▓▓▓▓▓▓▓▓▓▓▓▓▓▓▓▓▓▓▓▓▓▓▓▓▓▓
It is the policy ▓▓▓ of the City to hold prisoners ▓▓▓
▓▓▓▓▓▓▓ until ▓▓▓▓▓▓▓ extinguished
▓▓▓▓▓▓▓▓▓▓▓▓▓▓▓▓▓▓▓▓▓▓▓▓▓▓▓▓▓▓▓▓
It is the policy ▓▓▓▓▓▓▓▓▓▓▓▓▓▓▓▓▓▓▓▓
▓▓▓▓▓▓▓▓▓▓▓▓▓▓▓▓▓▓▓▓▓▓▓▓▓▓▓▓▓▓▓▓
▓▓▓▓▓▓▓▓▓▓▓▓▓▓▓▓▓▓▓▓▓▓▓▓▓▓▓▓▓▓▓▓
▓▓▓▓▓▓▓▓▓▓▓▓▓▓▓▓▓▓▓▓▓▓▓▓▓▓▓▓ It is
the policy ▓▓▓▓▓▓▓▓▓▓▓▓▓▓▓▓▓▓▓▓▓▓
▓▓▓▓▓▓▓▓▓▓▓▓▓▓▓▓▓▓▓▓▓▓▓▓▓▓▓▓▓▓▓▓
▓▓▓▓▓▓▓▓▓▓▓▓▓▓▓▓▓▓▓▓▓▓▓▓▓▓▓▓▓▓▓▓
▓▓▓ Plaintiffs seek ▓▓▓▓▓▓▓▓▓▓▓▓▓ relief

a 23-year-old woman   mother of two

police officers came

arrested her   she owed the City

Officers took   away   her two children

she   too poor to pay

told   she would   serve

taken   to   jail

Desperate to get back   children

labored to clean

jail bars

a 58-year-old disabled resident

arrested

took into custody

kept for three days

informed he would be released if someone pay

asked for mercy

The court

ordered him to serve 44 days

38-year-old father   lives
with   his children
                went to   police   after he
learned   he had   warrants   traffic tickets
                                arrested   placed in   jail
                            kept overnight
                                                        he owed
the City $1,600
                                                The judge
ordered him jailed
                                                        told
        released if he   served 23 days
                        told   he could   work off   his
debt

                did not want to clean
                                blood and feces   desperate
                agreed to clean   blood and feces from the jail floors
                                        lost his job while he sat in   jail

Montgomery Violated

Plaintiffs' rights by jailing them by threatening to jail them

Defendant's policy

violates the

Constitution   City   Violated

The City's policy

violates

Constitution

Request for Relief

WHEREFORE Plaintiffs request ⬛⬛⬛⬛⬛ relief ⬛⬛⬛⬛⬛⬛⬛⬛⬛⬛⬛⬛⬛⬛⬛⬛ equal protection ⬛⬛⬛⬛⬛⬛⬛⬛⬛⬛⬛ judgment ⬛⬛⬛ constitutional and statutory rights ⬛⬛⬛⬛⬛⬛⬛⬛⬛⬛⬛⬛ equal protection ⬛⬛⬛⬛⬛⬛⬛⬛⬛⬛⬛ judgment ⬛⬛⬛⬛⬛⬛⬛⬛⬛⬛⬛⬛⬛⬛⬛⬛⬛⬛⬛⬛⬛⬛⬛⬛⬛⬛⬛⬛⬛⬛⬛⬛ Fourth and Fourteenth Amendment rights ⬛⬛⬛⬛⬛⬛⬛⬛⬛⬛⬛⬛⬛⬛⬛⬛⬛⬛⬛⬛ A ⬛⬛⬛⬛ judgment ⬛⬛⬛⬛⬛⬛⬛⬛⬛⬛⬛⬛⬛⬛⬛⬛ due process ⬛⬛ equal protection ⬛⬛⬛⬛⬛⬛⬛⬛⬛⬛ rights ⬛⬛⬛⬛⬛⬛⬛

Respectfully submitted

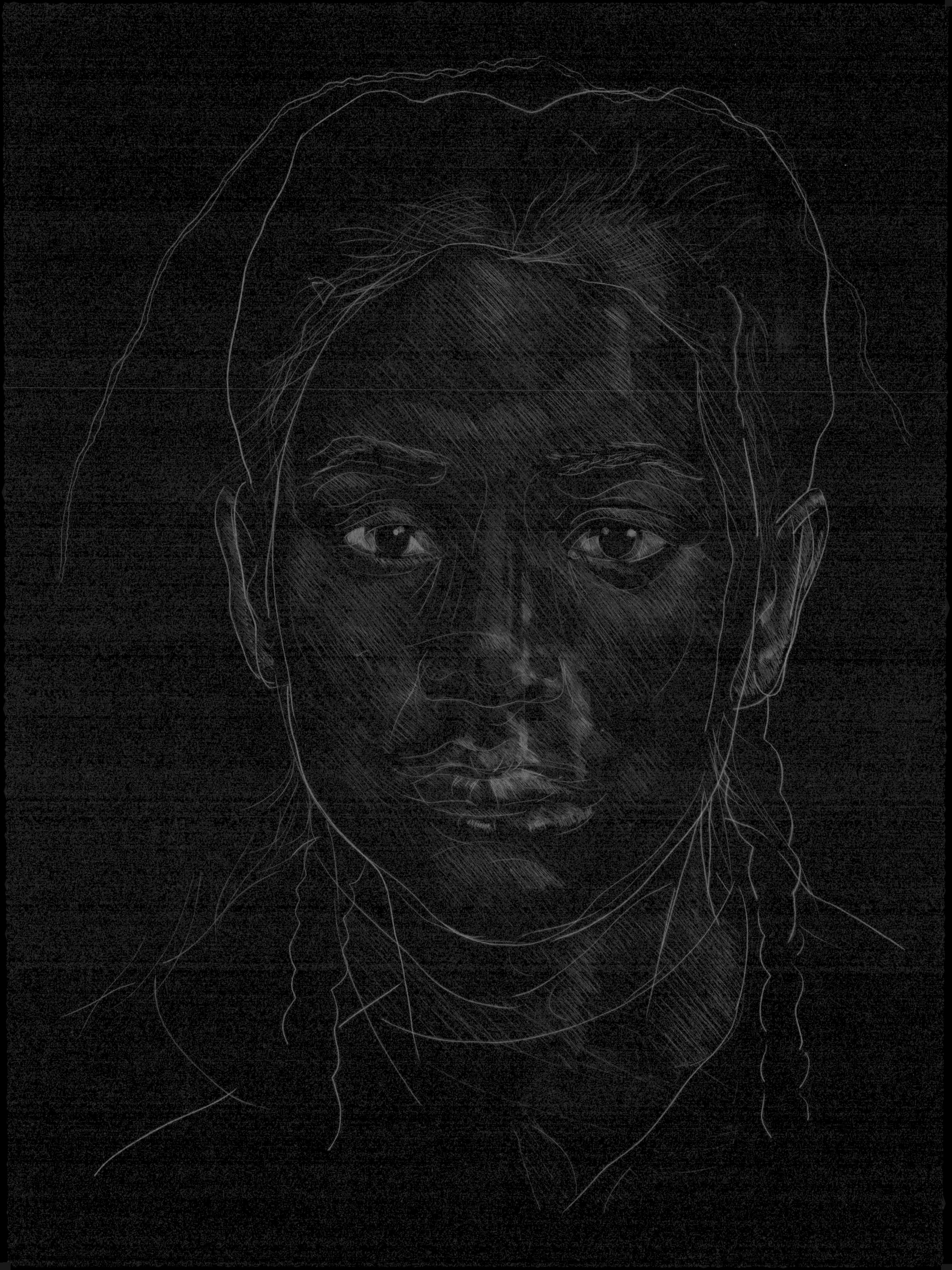

committed

federalist

Legislature

codified

oppression

The Fourteenth Amendment

Plaintiffs

law

radical jurisprudence

pleaded   Plaintiffs,

freedom

freedom

Plaintiffs

pleaded

Archive 2

We waited without a name,
With wonder, & after your birth,
After you entered this world,
Wailing like the dragons,
Your tiny hands reaching for light
At the hour of the jumbo jet, we
Waited & three days passed
Without words to announce this
Gift, & I read poems to myself,
& didn't think of the compass
I'd give you, years later, or
The compass you'd become
For me, & that afternoon, for
The first time, I was not lost,
Just discovering a story to tell
Myself about your brown eyes,
Aren't we always looking for
A story to tell ourselves? Whose
Name isn't shorthand for a myth?
We offered you a word in two
Tongues, the English a translation
For the Hebrew, or vice versa,
Each the name of your mother's
Older brother – the uncle you'll
Never meet, the names pulled
From the Book. Some wonder.
When I held you, your little body
Was neither wail nor howl, but
So fragile, & unafraid of these
Shivering hands or the lukewarm
Water of your first bath. You –
Light from your mother's belly,
Smiling then, as if to tell me,
Some of this song I sing is worthy.

Titus Kaphar and Reginald Dwayne Betts

Redaction

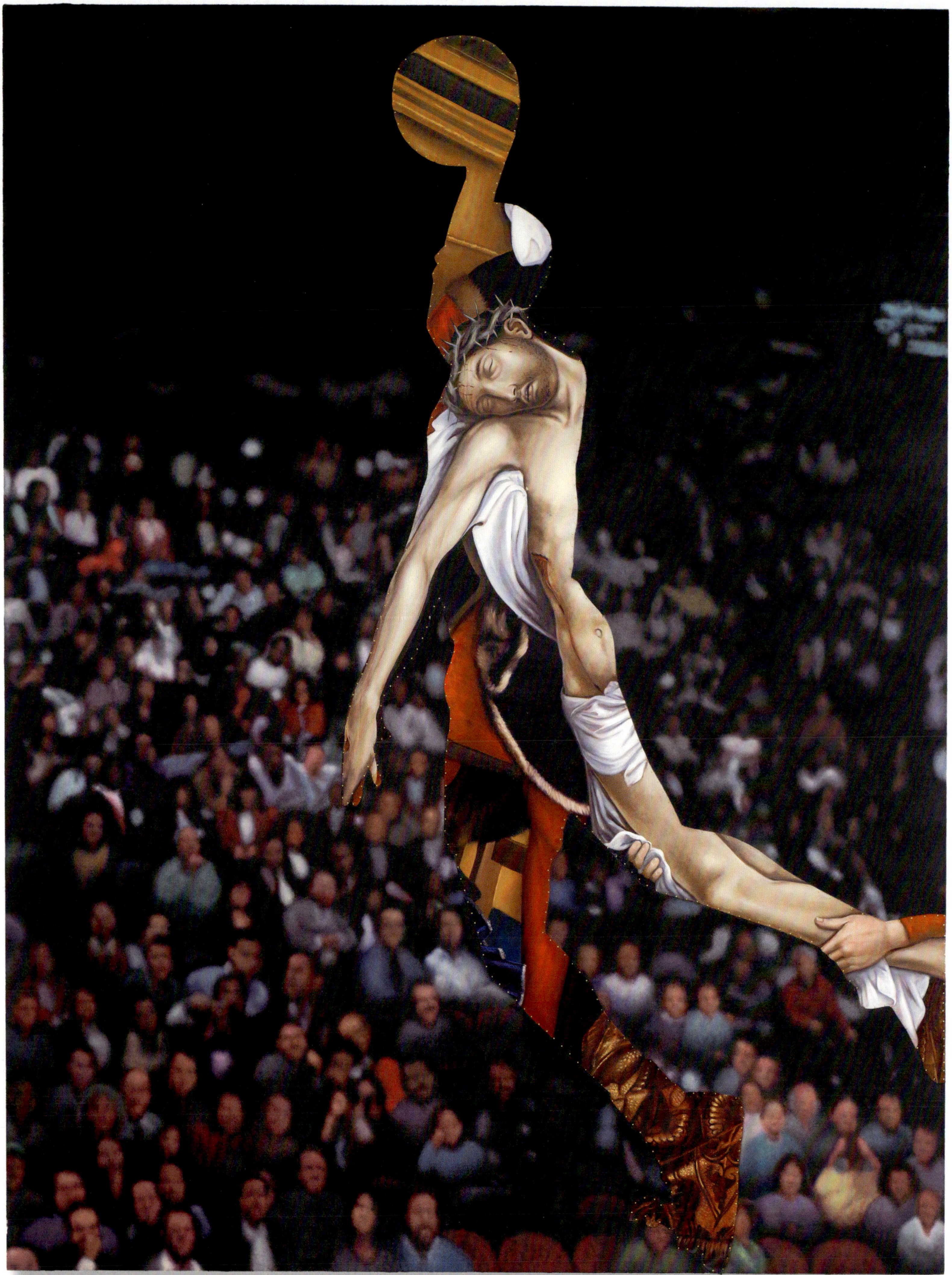

The late May day broke a record for cold
For us wanting to be anywhere but outside,
& it was the weekend we call Memorial,
My mother shipped off to the Iraq War a day
After her fiftieth birthday, but that is a story
For another time, & we were driving into
The mother of rivers state: my youngest,
Named after a man who turned a trumpet
Into a prayer, me, & friends who also believed
Watching their sons trade baskets with strangers
Was a kind of holy. Around us was more granite
Than Black folks & I carried Primo Levi's *If
This Is a Man* in my knapsack, hesitant to return
To all the astonishing ways we make each other
Suffer &, still, somehow, survive, & astonished
By how we remember. I've forgotten my share
Of things that matter. But who am I kidding?
The weekend was about basketball. We'd driven
Three hours to this colder weather. My youngest
Hoped he'd heat up once a ball graced his hands.
These were the days when he & the nine he suited
Up with desired little more than to hear the rasp
Of a ball against whatever passed for wood
In a gym with a hoop. There is something about
How basketball makes men of boys & boys
Of men. The other team had a player who made
Me think, though she be but little she is fierce,
As she, the only girl on the court, slipped a jewel
Into that hovering crown we cheered, even we
Whose boys sought to dribble & jump shot
Their way to the glory of a win. & when Miles
Came down as if he knew, I didn't hold my
Breath: a crossover, the ball then swung around
His back, the kid before him lost on some raft
In a wild river. Maybe Miles knew the ball would
Fall true because he turned to watch us as much
As to get back on defense. & we laughed & laughed
& laughed as kids barely large enough to launch
All of that need at a target did so, again & again.

This is how it happens, one morning
The ground is only the ground, & then
Green shoots through the rich brown loam.
I learned the word loam when I was starving
For something: fools would call it love,
& I would say it was a time machine, longing
For some days, months, years, when the sorrows
Didn't bloom like this thing from the ground
That I can barely name. Tell me how these
Peonies have migrated from Asia to my garden,
Have found their way into my line of vision
Despite prison & all the suffering I don't speak.
It all happens so sudden is what I mean to say,
When sadness becomes a beauty before your
Eyes so startling you ask friends what to name
This flower before you. I admit, I've pretended
To be g–d. To give a name to this thing that gives
Me joy. I called it Sunday, & then called it
After my firstborn. Have you ever been so rattled
By the unexpected. That you wanted someone's
Blessing to name the thing? The peonies are so
Lovely they frighten me. They grow on thin
Petioles that are longer than my arms with blooms
Heavier than the stems. But isn't it always so?
The beauty of the world so hefty we fear the world
Cannot stand it? & yet, why would we not want
To pray when we notice? Why do we forget that
Naming is the first kind of prayer, even as the white
Flowers turn into scented oil against my skin.

Redaction

Titus Kaphar and Reginald Dwayne Betts

Some mornings, after the sun has long set,
& the new day is still far enough away
That sleep feels inviting, night & silence,
Or the sound of your loves sleeping
Says more about tomorrow than the words
Of waking hours. Once, I wept at 3 a.m., standing
In the center of so many dreaming people
Who love me. I was warm from hurting
& the want for tomorrow & the want for one
More moment of just being there, listening
To them breathe away the night. How do you
Admit that you notice the world more when
You are alone in the noticing? When even nocturnal
Animals have retreated to the shadows? Wild, Yellow
daffodils are poisonous to humans & dogs
Alike. But only for those who believe beauty must
Be consumed. My loves sleep & all I want is
To know this moment, a kind of gratitude,
Witnessing what sustains me in the day,
Protected by the sleep that I'm denied at night.

You ask me how I'm doing
& I realize there are not enough
Words for joy in this language,
Not like the German, where a man
Can whisper a phrase for relief
That roughly translates to
It felt like a stone falling from
My heart, or Spanish, where to love
Is also to want. The g–ds must not
Know the things I've wanted in this
World. In prison, a letter is called
A kite, as if words alone can gift
A man wings. & I want to tell
You that my body is a kite
Swept into the wind, to say some
Days my heart is the wildest
Hungriest thing I know.
Whatever about choices,
Follow me now, the erratic thing
That knocks against my rib cage
Says. & I have, everywhere,
Off cliffs in cities whose names
I cannot pronounce, back into
Prisons, to my sons' basketball
Games, to weeping & to down on
My knees, to something I've
Never actually called joy, but
Just might be, that remembering
Of all the things I believed needed
Letting go, only to learn
The raft on which I ride into
My todays was built with them.

Titus Kaphar and Reginald Dwayne Betts

Redaction

Titus Kaphar and Reginald Dwayne Betts

It's so early in the morning that even
The birds sleep still, but my puppy
Awakens me with the thumping of her
Tail & foot & low bark against
Her crate. For independence's sake,
I must coax puppy from the small cave
Where she sleeps, whisper & coo
Until she comes into my arms & we
Go brave what is outside this house,
& though I didn't know it, I too must
Relieve myself, & though civilization
Says wait until I am back inside,
I long to go in a way I haven't since I
Was a child asleep in my mother's bed.
Has anyone admitted to you how a
Mother's warmth is so calming it makes
Not being afraid the easiest thing in
This madhouse of a century? The puppy
& I unburdened ourselves just as the first
Bird began to chirp. What a marvelous
Witness to the spectacle of my remembering—
Freedom is feeling unwatched, what a
Singular stunning song to accompany this
Vulnerability that reminds me of being loved.

At 2 a.m., without enough spirits
Spilling into my liver to call my tongue
To silence, my youngest learned the why
Of the years I spent inside a box: a spell,
A kind of incantation I was under; not whisky,
But History: As a teenager, I robbed a man,
I'd tell him months before he would drop
Bucket after bucket on opposing players,
The bedraggled bunch five & six & he leaping
As if every layup erases something. That's how
I saw it, my screaming-coaching-sweating
Presence recompense for the pen. My father
Has never seen me play ball is part of this.
My oldest knew, brought into this truth by
A stranger. Tell me we aren't running toward
Failure is what I want to ask him, but it is 2
In the a.m. & he has gone off to dream in
The comfort of his room, the youngest, despite
Seeming more lucid than me; just reflects cartoons
Back from his eyes. & so, when he tells me,
Daddy it's okay, I know what's happening is some
Straggling angel, lost from his pack finding
A way to fulfill his duty, lending words
To this kid who crawls into my arms, wanting,
More than stories of my prisons, the sleep
That he fought while I held court at a bar with
Men who knew that when the drinking was over,
The drinking wouldn't make the stories
We brought home any easier to tell.

Redaction

Redaction 2

IN

HOUSTON
_____

et al

v

HARRIS COUNTY TEXAS et al

_____

JUDGES MOTIONS TO DISMISS

Bail   Plaintiffs seek to abolish

bail

to challenge

Texas

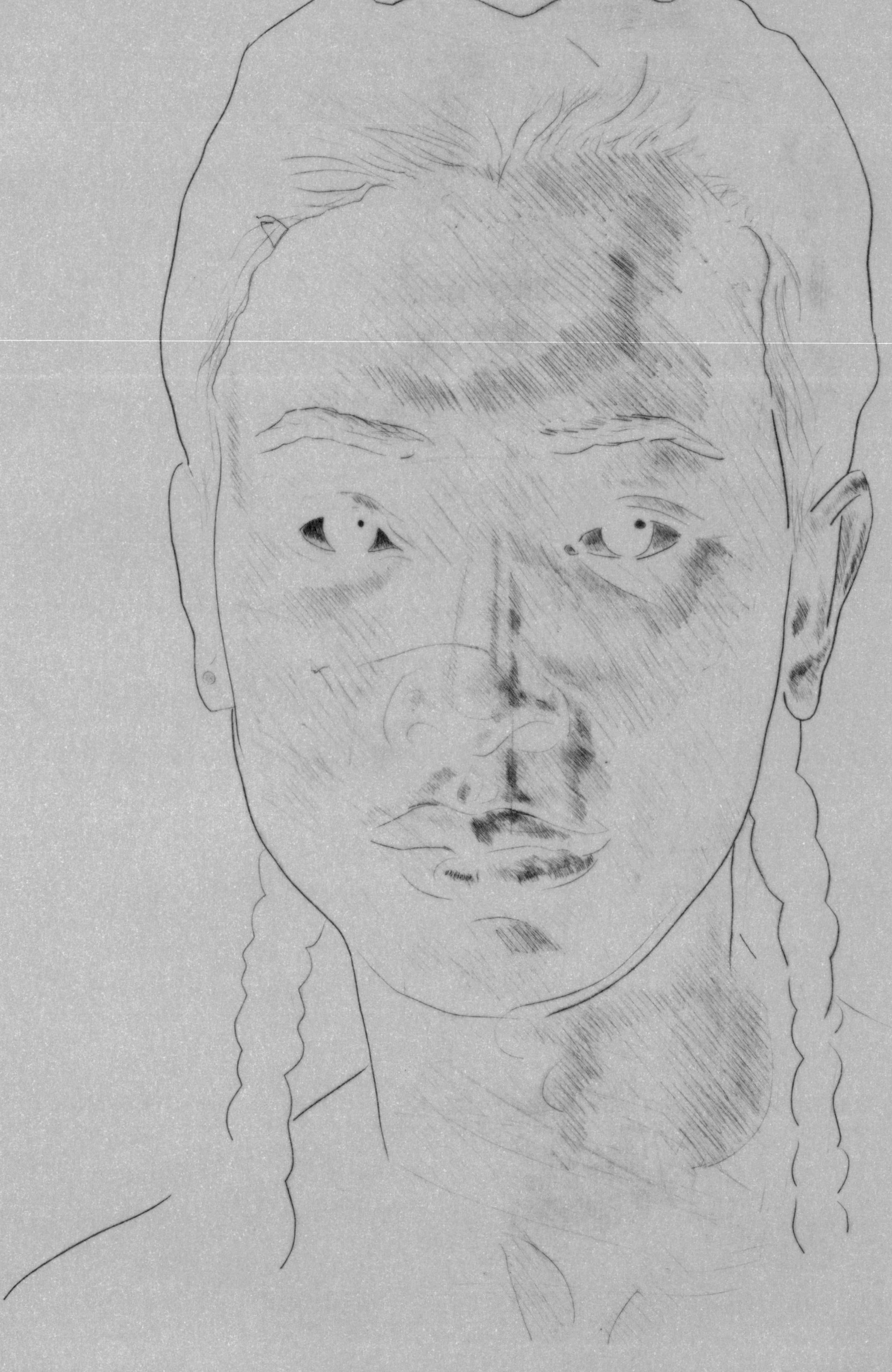

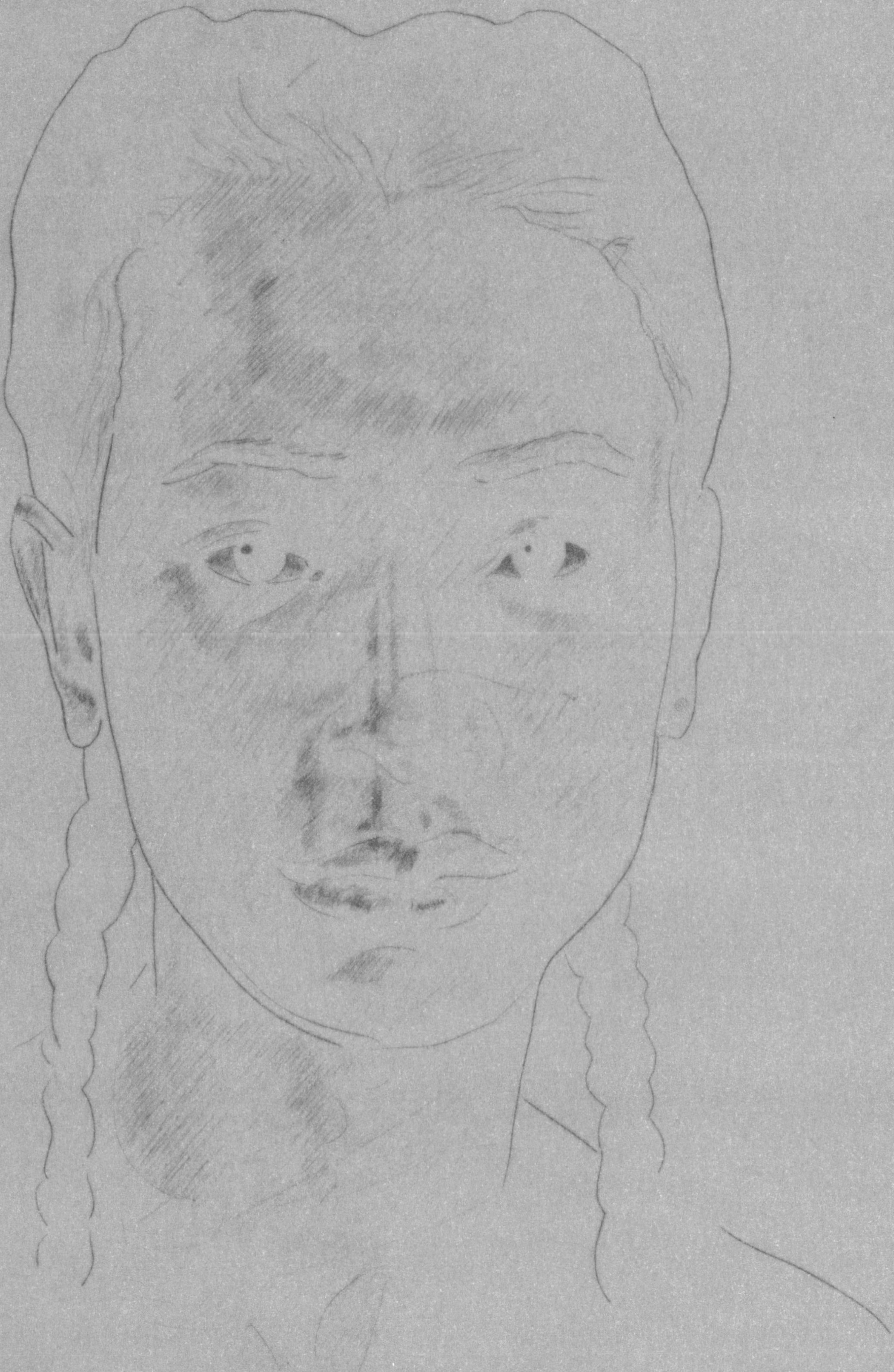

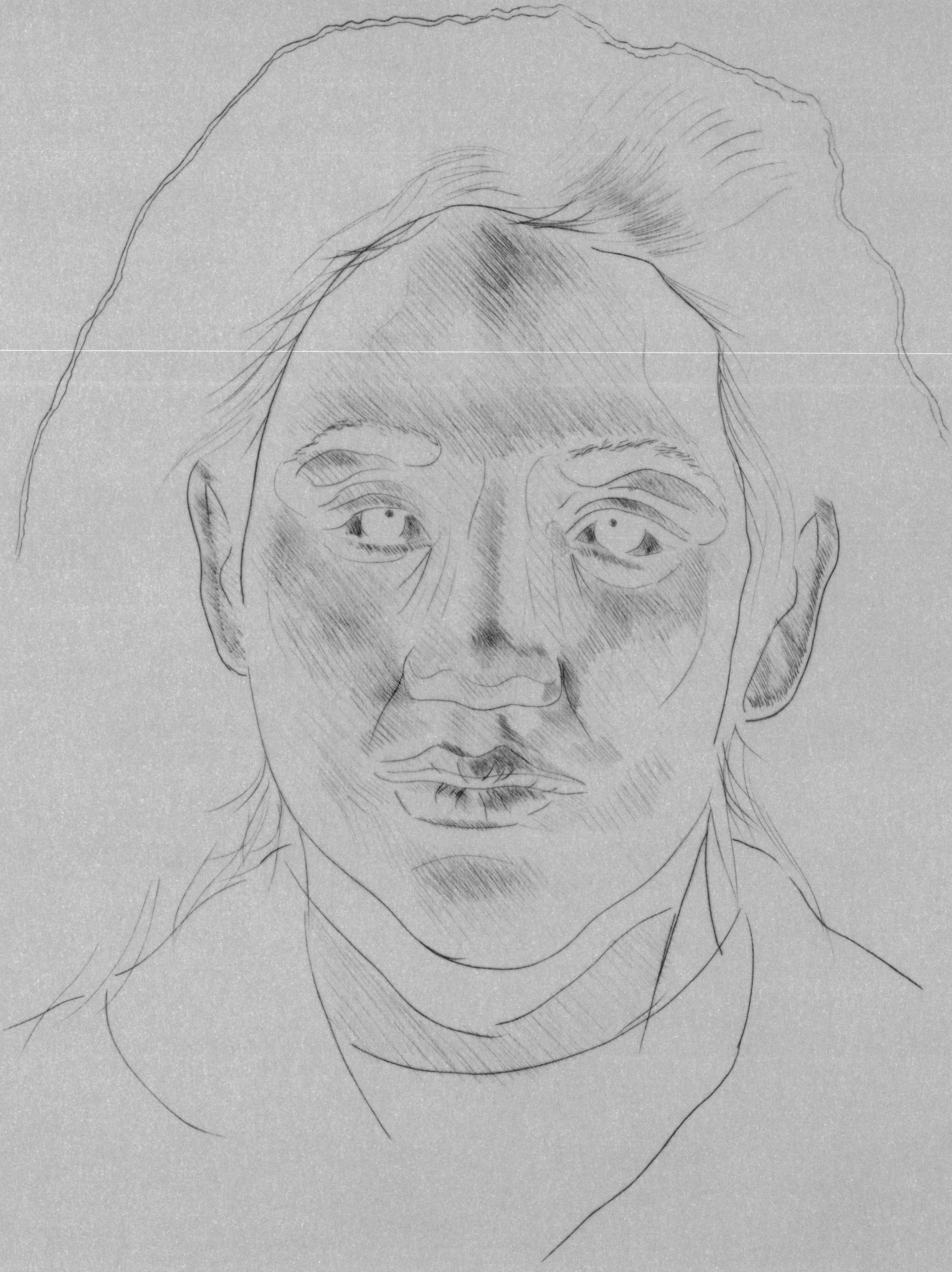

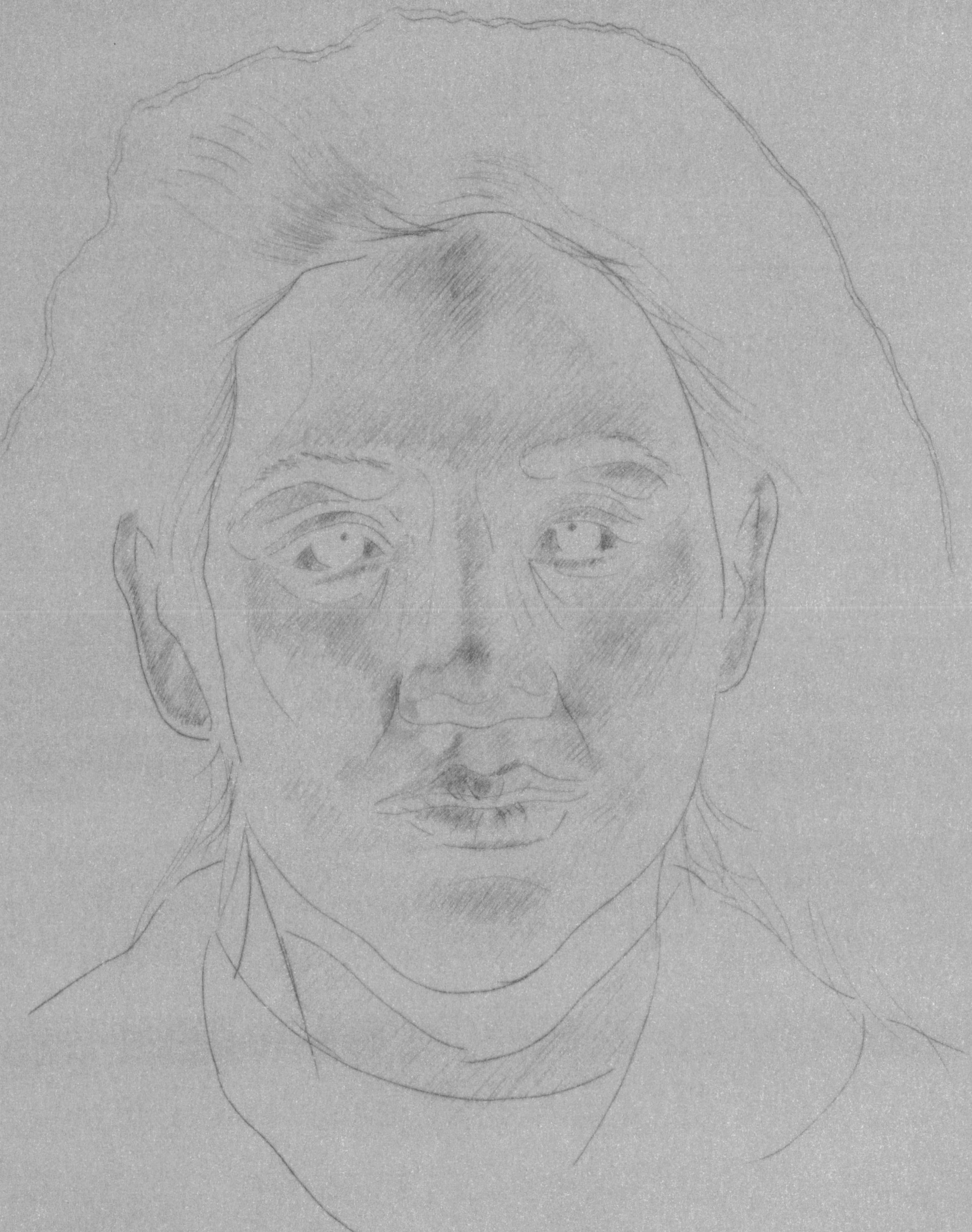

IN ▬▬▬▬▬▬▬
HOUSTON ▬▬▬▬▬

▬▬▬▬▬▬ et al
▬▬▬

v

HARRIS COUNTY TEXAS et al
▬▬▬▬ ▬▬▬▬▬

▬▬▬▬▬▬▬ JUDGES MOTIONS TO DISMISS
▬▬▬▬▬▬▬▬▬▬▬

▬▬▬▬▬▬▬▬▬▬▬▬▬▬▬▬
▬▬▬▬▬▬

Bail ▬▬▬ Plaintiffs seek to abolish ▬▬▬▬▬
▬▬▬▬▬▬▬▬▬▬▬▬▬▬▬▬
bail ▬▬▬▬▬▬▬▬▬▬▬
▬▬▬▬▬▬▬▬▬▬▬▬▬▬▬▬
▬▬ ▬▬▬ to challenge ▬▬▬▬▬▬▬▬
▬ ▬▬▬▬ ▬▬▬▬ Texas ▬▬▬▬▬▬
▬▬

Plaintiffs allege   bail

is unconstitutional   because it fails

allege

the Eighth Amendment

ignore the

constitution

These claims should be dismissed

These challenges

should be dismissed

Plaintiffs seek to federalize

Harris County This is antithetical to our

past Plaintiffs   demand

the Court abandon

bail

Plaintiffs core complaint is is nothing resoundingly and repeatedly rejected Plaintiffs seek to invent the Fourteenth Amendment Plaintiffs equal protection claim fails

bail

been recognized since the eighteenth century

bail

is and was constitutional

Plaintiff

lacks standing she is a fugitive

Plaintiff lacks

standing he was in jail

Plaintiff lacks

standing

Plaintiffs alleges

Equal Protection

Plaintiffs allege

Plaintiffs claim

Plaintiffs allege

Plaintiffs allege

Plaintiffs claim

Bail originated   400 years ago

The issue is not novel   litigated since the beginning

bail is not unconstitutional

Plaintiffs propose a radical

jurisprudence

Under this view

the Fourteenth

Amendment would   overrule

the Eighth Amendment

The Fourteenth Amendment   the Eighth

Amendment

the Eighth Amendment

the Fourteenth Amendment

Pursuant to our federalist system the

defendants

must be

used as   an instrument of oppression

This system exists to   prejudice

the

bail system
has proven   an extremely effective tool

some criminal defendants   remain   despite being able to bail out

the defendant   their contacts
chosen not to post bond due to health

parent wants to stop drug use or the defendant wishes to remain the jail provides shelter multiple meals per day medical services

Plaintiffs' claims should be dismissed Plaintiffs are asking Court to intervene

Plaintiffs' claims should also be dismissed Judges are not the creators of bail

the Judges are immune from damages

In ▇▇▇ the State of California
▇▇▇

In re ▇▇▇ ▇▇▇
▇▇
▇

Petition for Writ of Habeas Corpus

▇▇▇▇▇▇▇▇▇▇
▇▇▇▇▇

▇▇ arrested ▇▇
▇▇ a 63-year-old man a retired shipyard laborer ▇ a lifelong resident ▇▇ arrested ▇ charged ▇ first degree residential robbery ▇▇ first degree residential burglary ▇▇ inflicting injury ▇▇ on elder ▇ ▇▇▇ theft ▇▇ ▇▇ not ▇ a capital offense ▇▇ no ▇▇▇ threat of great bodily harm ▇

defense requested release

advanced age

lifelong resident of San Francisco

shipyard laborer

lack of a recent criminal

prosecutor requested $600,000 money bail a criminal protective order

The judge denied release set bail $600,000 The court emphasized public safety

$600,000

did not have money to pay

argued ▬▬ bail ▬▬ beyond his means ▬▬ violated the Fourteenth Amendment's ▬▬ the Eighth Amendment's ▬▬ prosecution argued ▬▬ public safety ▬▬ flight risk concerns ▬▬ prosecutor requested ▬▬ detention ▬▬ court denied ▬▬ request

████████████████████████████

████████ presented ████████ acceptance letter

███ Golden Gate for Seniors ████████

asked to be released ████████ to Golden Gate

████████ emphasized ███ advanced age ██

████████████████

treatment for ██ battle with addiction ███

████████████████

too poor to pay the cash ████

████████████████

████████████████

████████████

██ petitioner asks ███ A writ of habeas corpus be issued ████

████████ ordering ██████ released ████

████████ an expedited hearing ██

███ the court inquire into ████████

ability to pay ████████████ release

██ not ████ to detain him ████ release ████████

████████████ release

Archive 3

I was in a city where everything juxtaposes
With everything else. My hat anchored
The bar's end, the Brunswick green,
The shimmering feathers that at once
Were oil slick black & almost iridescent,
The thin one, with its white dots & streaks
Of red, the wide brim. I wonder if, on my
Head, it turns me into what I am, a man
Who desires to be noticed. The feathers remind
Me of a bird I know — a greater sage grouse,
For four weeks a year its mundane patchwork
Of wings become plumage, a fan of wonder
& delight & the hope that another grouse will
Want to be folded into that adornment. Who
Hasn't followed some desperation to be lovely
In this world that measures losses in monuments.
I know grouse also means to complain & be petty.
That's how words do, in one language, the beautiful
Thing longing to be seen comes from the Latin
For crane, in another such a desire translates
Into bellyaching. My plumage has become
A lament of cell doors closing. The liquor I drink
Is as brown as my skin & may be turning my liver
Into a crime scene. & yes, the feathers in my hat
Are more feint than truth. The rest matters little.
Sometimes your sins make you want to vanish,
Unsettled by how there may be no song without them.

Redaction

Titus Kaphar and Reginald Dwayne Betts

& flowers I cannot name, & this heart,
That science says weighs 231 grams,
Of which would fit in my hand,
This hand that has held a pistol (once),
& two children who call me mother.
The flowers make me wonder about
Beauty, how a year ago I'd not known
They existed, in the same way the heart's
Ventricles confuse me, that entire engine
Of beauty & joy. I'm so much better
At knowing the things I've held in my hands,
So much better at expecting those loves.
But my g–d, when the flowers erupt from
The earth in surprises of pink & purple
& red & something an old lover once called
Viridescent, the locked box in my chest
Flutters, & I am surprised when these
Lovely things call back my first kiss.

There is the dream, & then there is a moment
When morning comes with a combination
Of colors that have never existed before,
The vernacular calls this dawn, or first light,
Or sunup, daybreak, break of day, cockcrow,
Aurora, there are so many words for
This particular beauty, & no one dare call
It fleeting, this beginning, this kind of horse
We ride into what we hope will happen,
This strange & wild thing that gallops us to our life.

Redaction

Titus Kaphar and Reginald Dwayne Betts

My father wants forgiveness
& his desire makes me know
That love is to be willing
To carry the water for another.
& in the morning, here, against
The bluest sky, I see the only
Burden I've known: forgetfulness.
& it's strange how belief reminds,
Makes you know the murmuration
Of starlings & their beating wings,
Might easily be your own heart,
& of course you will fly, of course
You've always been flying.

You forget America's stories? Then behold this process:
How we avoid letting anyone pigeonhole this process.

My g–d, what's left when all the weeping's done?
Whose mother believes art will console this process?

In museums, only the guards looked like his kin —
Why would Kaphar let the market control this process?

My brother said you and your man mastered the hustle,
I told him only our sweat would bankroll this process.

Materials: tar & regret, what others would forget,
A knife against canvas, ready to charcoal this process.

Maybe it's the tension between the world & me,
Should I reveal this Black soul? This process?

Our journey through words & images meant to trouble;
Shahid & Titus, refuse to let them blackhole this process.

Redaction 3

IN   MISSOURI

_____

                              et al

v

THE CITY OF FERGUSON

_____

                The Plaintiffs   people   jailed by
the City

                                                the City kept a human

        in its jail   the person

                       pleaded   poverty

    held   indefinitely

                                                    threatened abused

    left to languish   frightened

family members could   buy their freedom

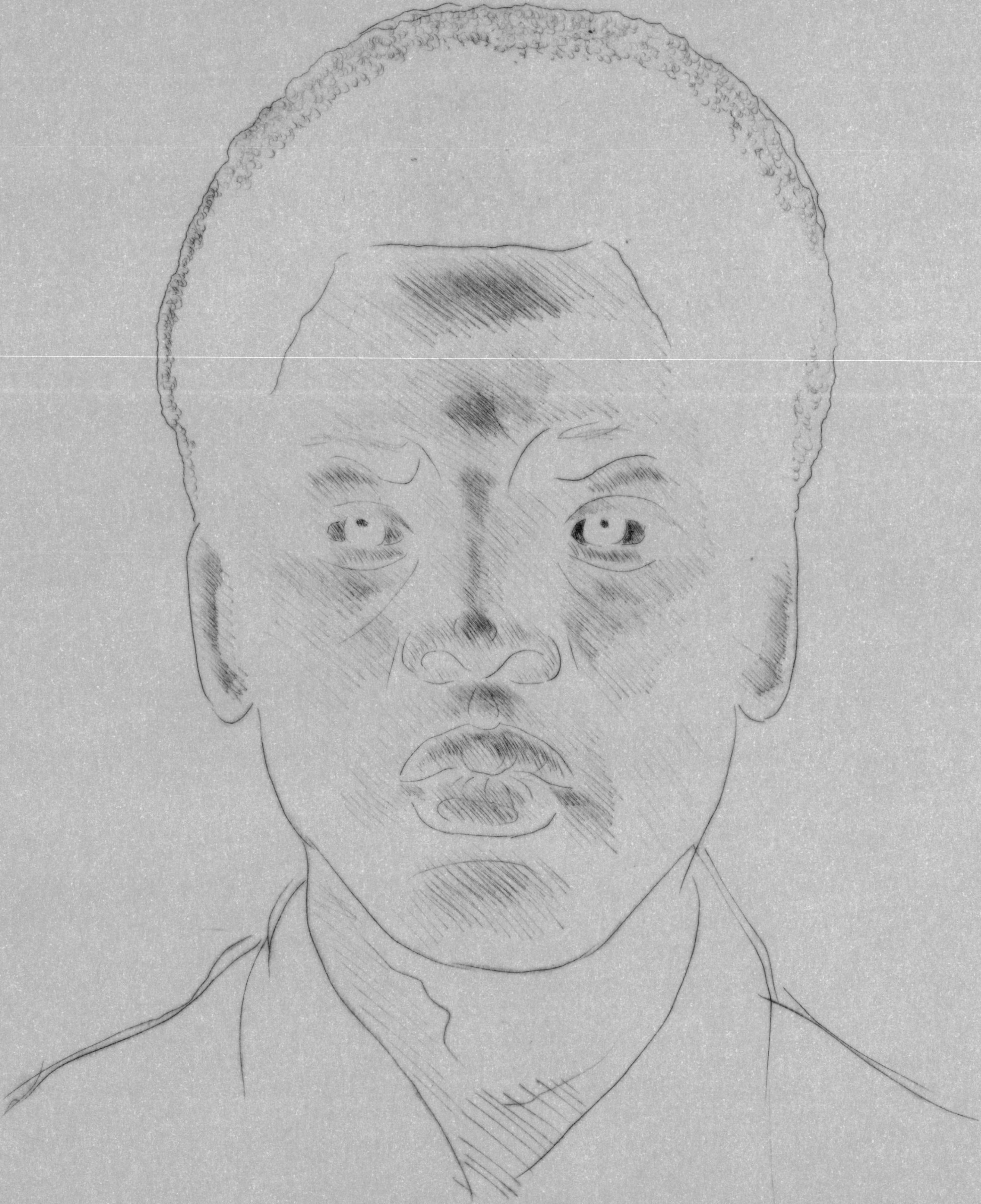

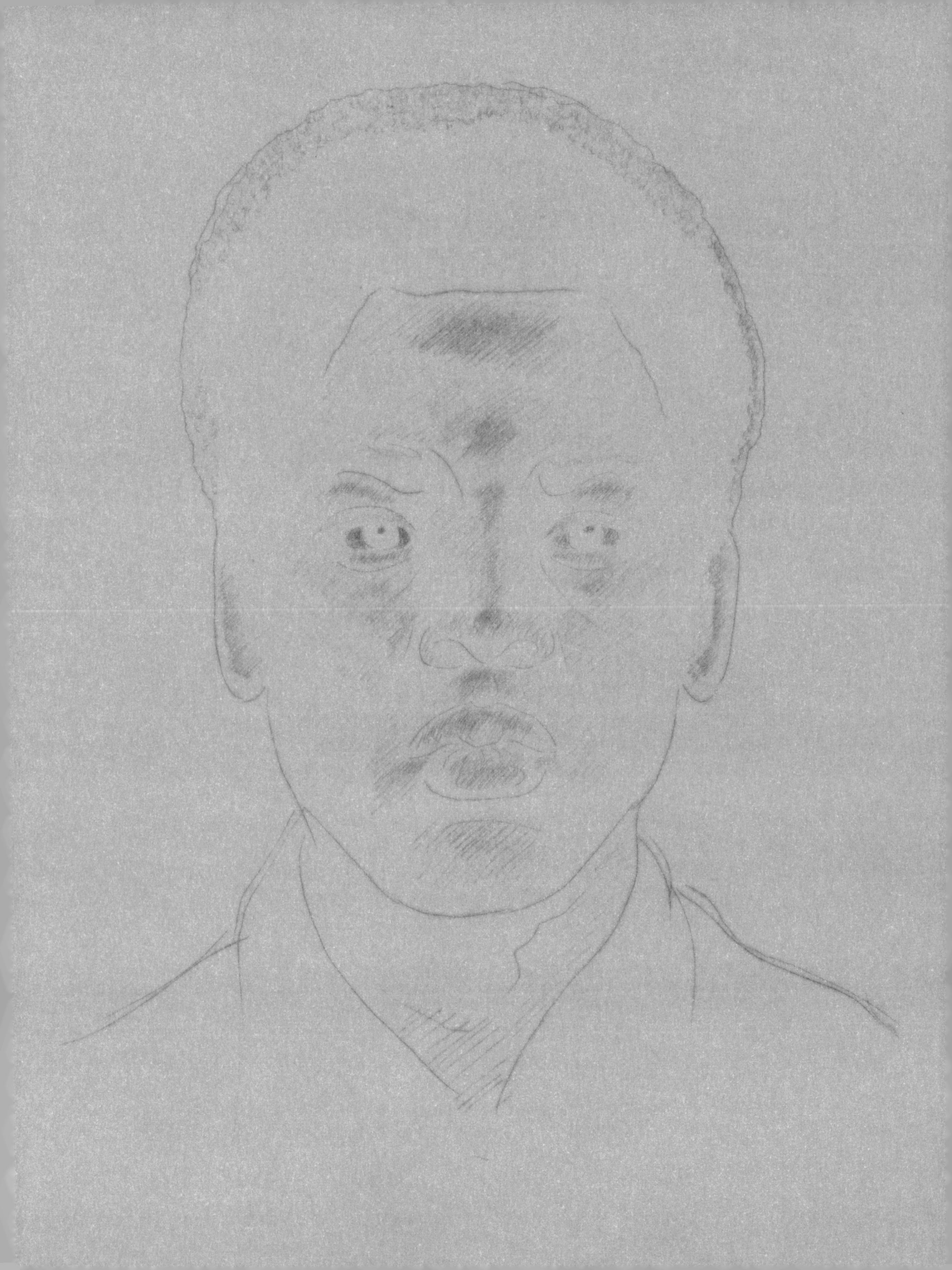

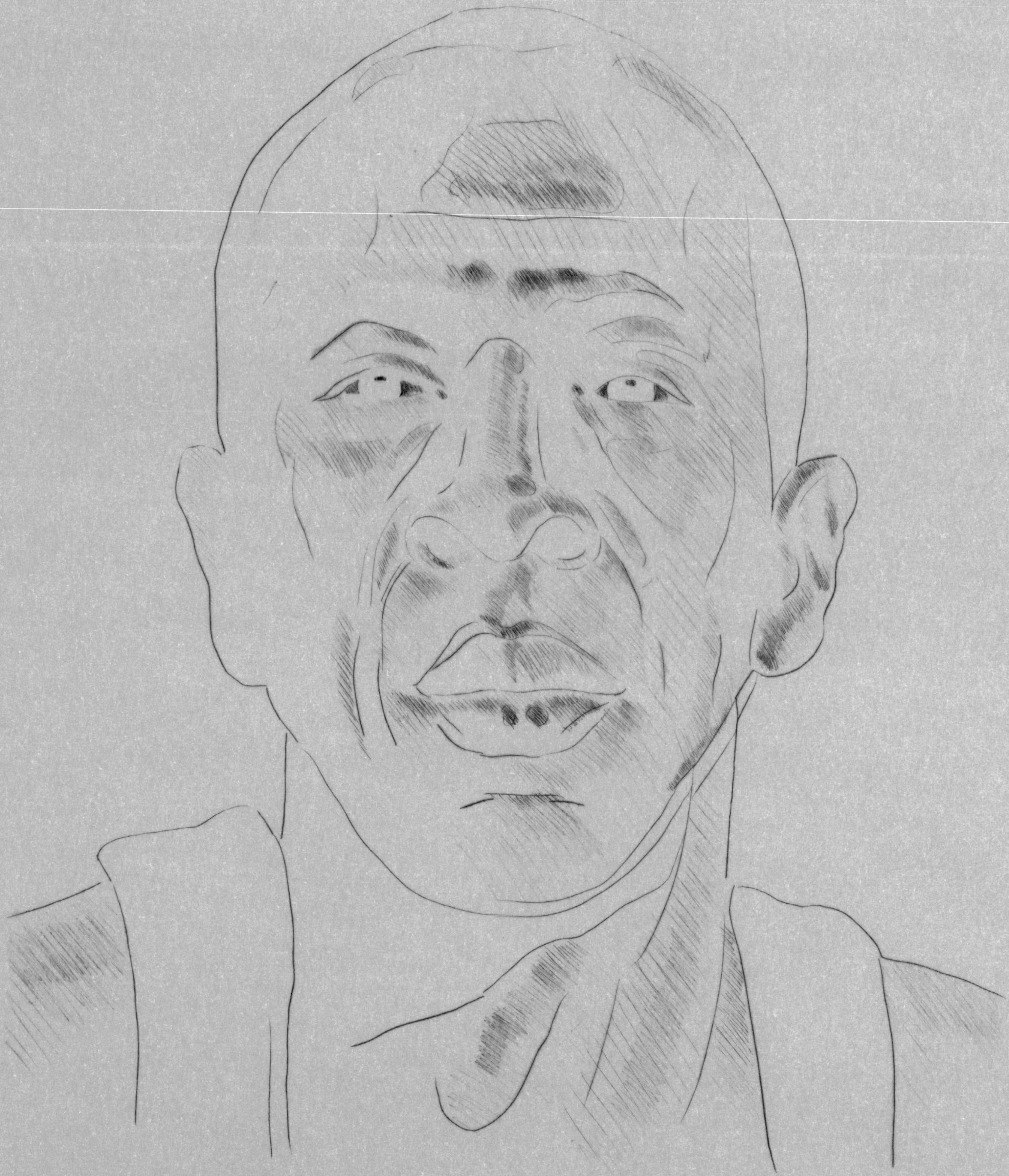

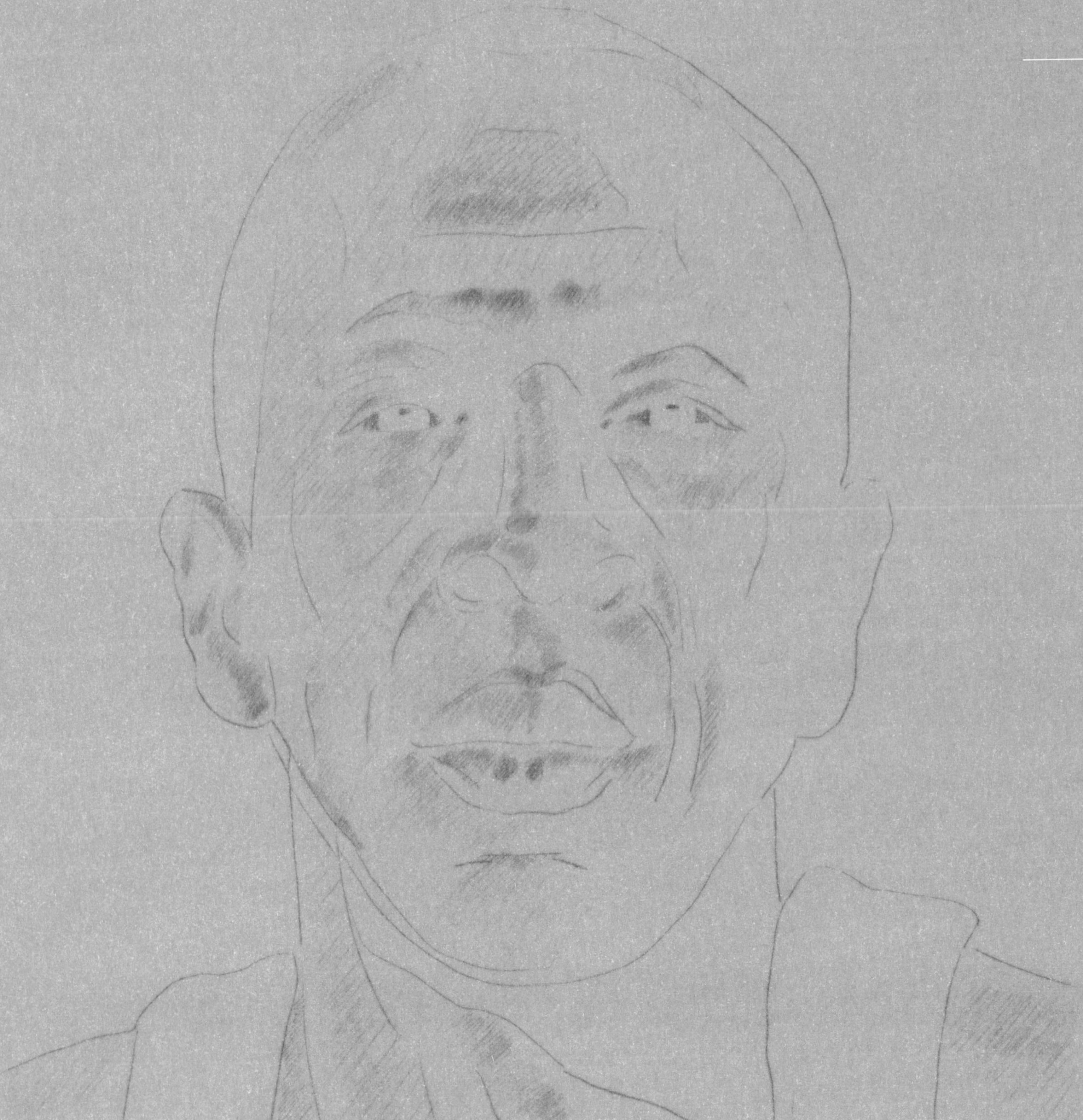

IN
                                                                              MISSOURI

█████ et al

v

THE CITY OF FERGUSON

                    The Plaintiffs   people   jailed by
the City
                                                              the City kept a human
   in its jail   the person
                   pleaded   poverty
   held   indefinitely
                                                                   threatened abused
   left to languish   frightened
family members could   buy their freedom

impoverished   cannot
endure grotesque treatment   overcrowded cells
denied toothbrushes toothpaste   soap   subjected to the   stench
of excrement and refuse   surrounded by walls smeared
with mucus and blood   for days and weeks
                                                    bodies
cover   the entire   cell floor
                       untreated illnesses   infections in open wounds
                       days   weeks
              filthy bodies huddle in cold   a single thin
blanket

they   lose
           weight they suffer
                                              they must listen
to the screams   they sit
       without   natural light
                   when they will be allowed to leave

These physical abuses

Jail guards taunt people

jail guards

laugh humiliate them

shivering women forced to
share blankets officers shout stanky ass
dykes dirty whores
City officials employees

built a scheme
designed to brutalize to punish to profit The architect

the City of Ferguson

The City of Ferguson

the rest of the Saint Louis

modern debtors prison

the City of Ferguson

devastated the City's poor trapping them in

debts extortion and cruel jailings

The treatment

reveals systemic illegality

The City has

a

a

Dickensian system that   violates the

most vulnerable

the City of Ferguson

the

City's conduct is unlawful

It   has been the policy   to jail

people

the   practice   to jail indigent

the   practice   to hold prisoners

indefinitely

the   practice   to issue

invalid   warrants to threaten

to hold arrestees in jail

arbitrarily

to confine

people   in grotesque dangerous and

inhumane conditions a Kafkaesque journey

a lawless and labyrinthine scheme of

perpetual debt

These physical abuses

Jail guards taunt people

jail guards

laugh humiliate them

shivering women forced to

share blankets officers shout stanky ass

dykes dirty whores

City officials employees

built a scheme

designed to brutalize to punish to profit The architect

the City of Ferguson

The City of Ferguson

the rest of the Saint Louis

modern debtors prison

the City of Ferguson

devastated the City's poor trapping them in

debts extortion and cruel jailings

The treatment

reveals systemic illegality

The City has

a

a

Dickensian system that   violates the

most vulnerable

the City of Ferguson

the

City's conduct is unlawful

It   has been the policy   to jail

people

In the State of California

In re

Petition for Writ of Habeas Corpus

arrested

a 63-year-old man a retired shipyard laborer   a lifelong resident   arrested   charged

first degree residential robbery   first degree residential burglary   inflicting injury   on elder

theft

not   a capital offense   no

threat of great bodily harm

parent wants   to stop drug use
or the defendant wishes to remain   the
jail provides shelter multiple meals per day   medical services

Plaintiffs claims

should be dismissed

Plaintiffs are asking   Court to intervene

Plaintiffs' claims

should also be dismissed

Judges are not the creators of   bail

the   Judges

are   immune from

damages

defense requested release

advanced age

lifelong resident of San Francisco

shipyard laborer

lack of a recent criminal

prosecutor requested $600,000   money bail   a criminal

protective order

The judge denied   release   set   bail

$600,000   The court

emphasized public safety

$600,000

did not have   money to

pay

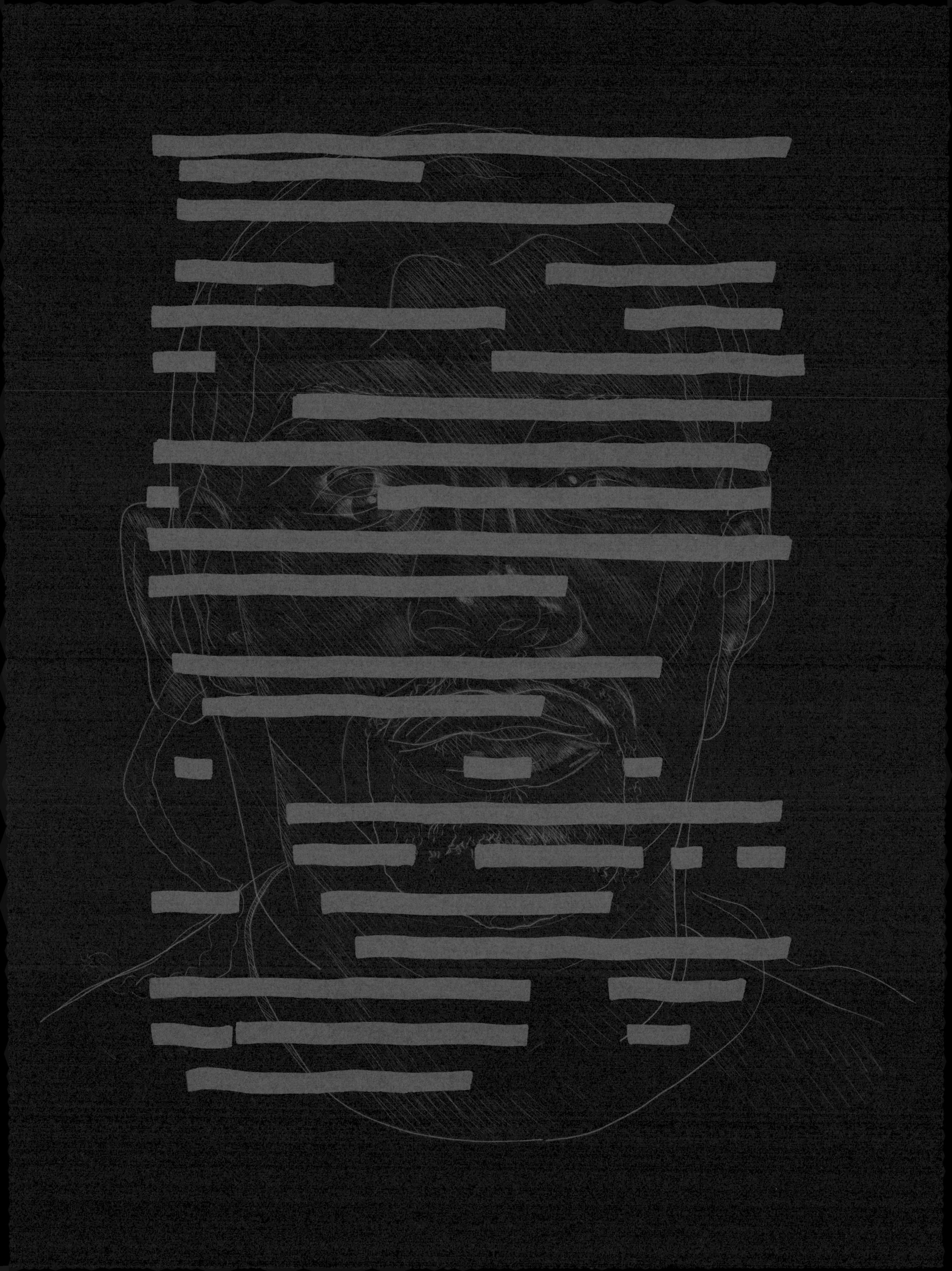

bail   beyond his means   violated the Fourteenth   argued

Amendment's

the Eighth Amendment's

prosecution argued

public safety   flight risk concerns   prosecutor

requested   detention   court denied

request

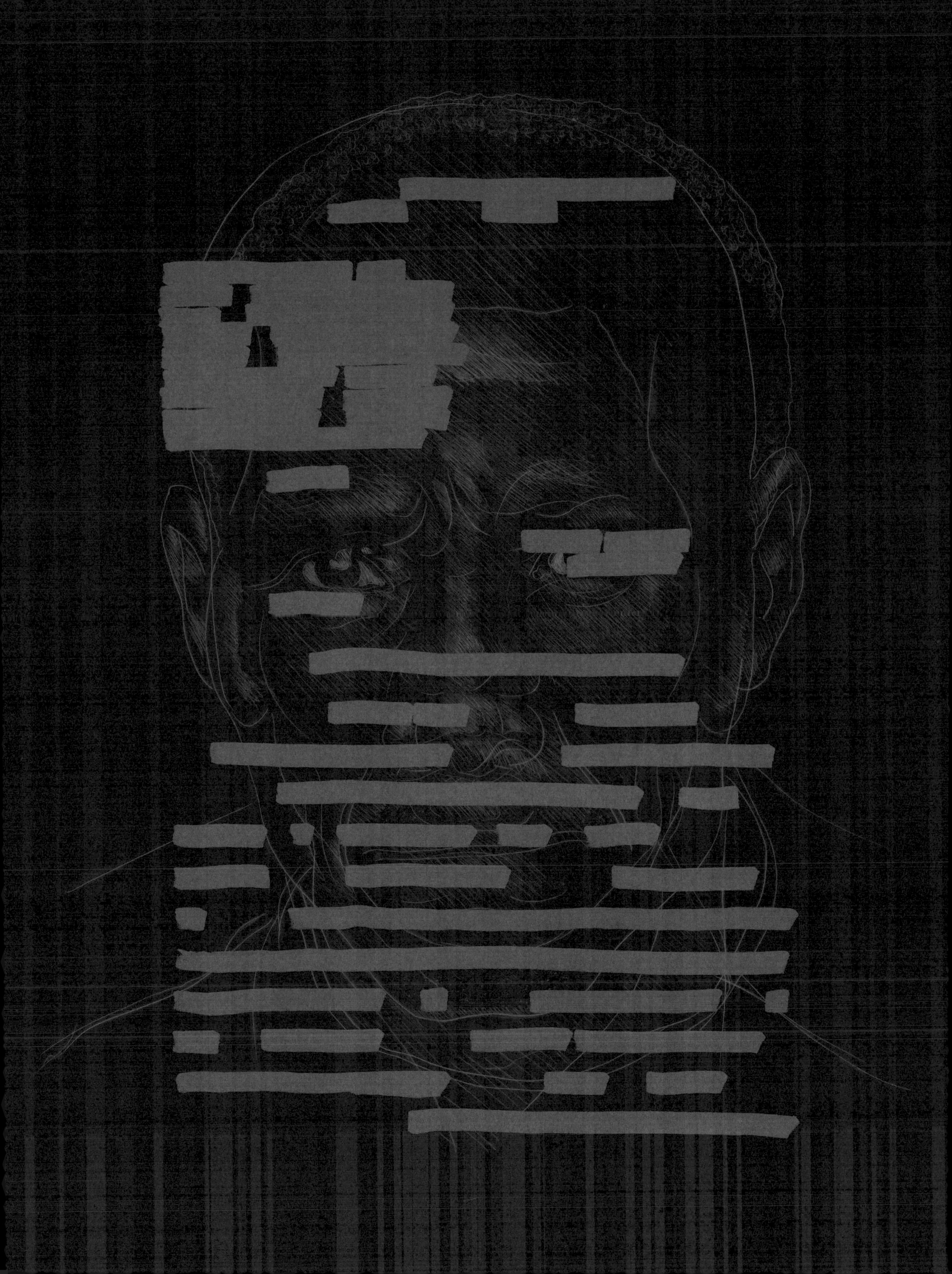

IN THE MIDDLE OF ALABAMA
_____

v

THE CITY OF MONTGOMERY
_____

The Plaintiffs impoverished jailed by the City unable to pay traffic tickets pay or sit in jail $50 per day Plaintiffs unable to pay each sent to jail

told they could work off debts $25 per day cleaning the City scrubbing feces and blood from jail floors

oppression

The Fourteenth Amendment

Plaintiffs

law

radical jurisprudence

Habeas
Corpus

shipyard
laborer

63-year-old man

retired

This brother is dancing in the city,
His bald head the only sun some of us
Will see on this winter day, his body
Draped in the colors of heaven,
& each limb living in every borough
At once. How I've wanted to be free.
When I tell my son about this brother,
& how a scar from his forehead to his lip
Was not nearly the most interesting thing
About him, I think of his feet, & wonder
How to be that kind of honest: inventing,
Within the moment, everything that matters.
I want to be somebody's child again,
& young enough to stand before a mirror
Until my body memorizes moves I believe may
Save me. Maybe nothing saves us, save
Being witness to someone else moving so free.

Black Matter

Forest Young and Jeremy Mickel
Redaction Typeface: A Multiplicity of Typographic, Legal, and Human Histories

Redaction is a bespoke typeface commissioned by Titus Kaphar and Reginald Dwayne Betts's *Redaction* exhibition at MoMA PS1. As part of a timely conversation at the intersection of history, the legal system and social justice, the fonts will be free for personal use. In a spirit of generosity, the artists invite everyone to broaden the ethos of the exhibition by making these tools accessible to a global and engaged audience.

The *Redaction* project seeks to highlight the abuses in the criminal justice system, in particular the way poor and marginalized people are imprisoned for failure to pay court fines and fees. When Titus Kaphar and Reginald Dwayne Betts began their collaboration on *Redaction*, they identified that typography should be an important extension of the work. This emphasis on text and legibility presented a unique design opportunity: to create a bespoke typeface that could be used in the work, and also serve as a scalable tool to raise awareness of the project and reach even more people. To fulfill the typographic potential of the project, Kaphar reached out to Forest Young, a colleague from Yale, now Global y are afforded a hearing to argue for their release. H

ased from jail depends entirely on her access to money

2. Pursuant to this discriminatory scheme, in

gths of time. ==How long presumptively innocent arrest==

whether they or their families are able to pay, to borrov

==ird-party surety.== Others, like Mr. Hester, who are too

ay the secured money bond for them, remain in jail for

3. Mr. Hester was arrested on ==July 27, 2017,==

aphernalia and is currently incarcerated because he c

uired by the bail schedule. If he could pay the am

Highlighter emphasizes text

Pursuant to Rule 33.1(b

accompanying Brief for Respor

Municipal Employees, Council

12-point typeface, contains 14,

that are exempted by Rule 33.

word-count function of the wor

All text treated equally

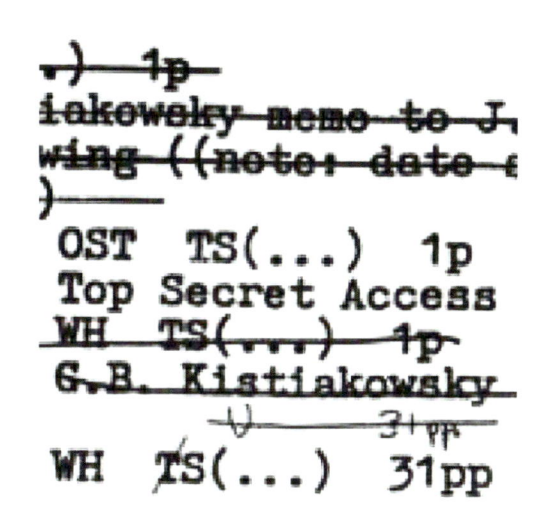

~~.) 1p~~
~~iakowsky memo to J.~~
~~wing ((note: date~~
~~)~~

OST TS(...) 1p
Top Secret Access
~~WH   TS(...)   1p~~
~~G.B. Kistiakowsky~~
~~.)   3+pp~~

WH   TS(...)   31pp

Strikethrough deemphasizes
text, but still legible

2. Forwarded as A
a placed to and fro
2 November. Analy
ovember and the mo
ed no pertinent inf

3. [Technical] surv
suspected Soviet in
information.

4. Forwarded as A

Text redacted, but still
possible to read

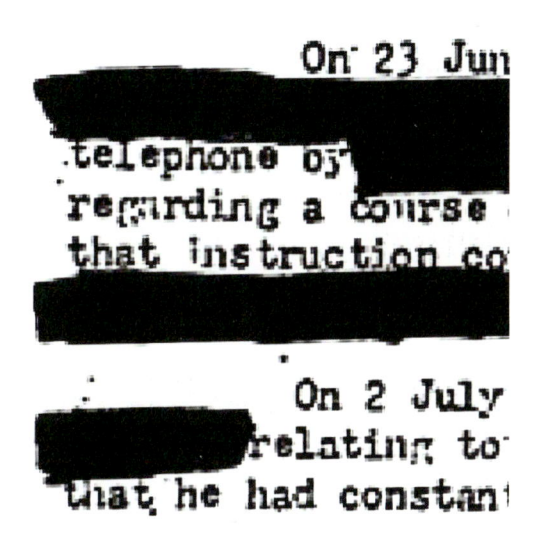

On 23 Jun
▮▮▮▮telephone o▮
▮regarding a course
▮that instruction co▮
▮▮▮▮▮▮▮▮▮

On 2 July
▮▮relating to
that he had constan

Complete redaction of text

complaints submi

2011. We have no

the Santa Ana Jail

York County Pris

in Kenosha, Wisc

complaints which

(Theo Lacy).

Bitmap from fax

MEMORANDU

SUBJECT: JTF

1. On 14 Decem

of JTF GTMO S

Bulking / distortion
from photocopying

ABSTRACT:
last Novemb
cation of v
of COSMIC,
Stolyarov.
cation meth

Degradation from photographing
faint historical material

al Effect
Survival ti
Genetic Eff
Histopatholo
Physiologica
Biochemical

Coarse bitmap from
high-speed scanning

Redaction Typeface

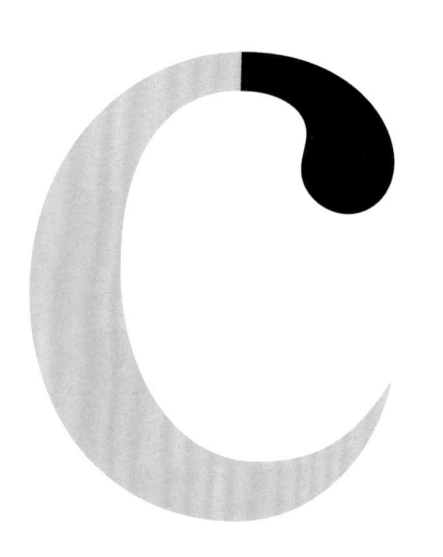

The arrows and olive branch "cruelty and compassion" dichotomy found on the Great Seal of the United States informed the Redaction font's letterforms with a mix of round and razor-sharp shapes.

Head of Brand at Rivian, who in turn recruited Jeremy Mickel, type designer and owner of MCKL.

The first phase of the project consisted of research and immersion. It was imperative to learn as much as possible about the history and nature of legal documents, and the various approaches to redaction. Unsurprisingly, the designers found a spectrum of redaction: forms extending beyond the simple black box — an incomplete redaction; stamps marked "deleted" but not obscuring the text; white boxes that appeared to invite the user to fill in their own text, and ad hoc hand-made notations, among others.

Specifically, the team noted that the vast majority of legal documents in the United States followed a set convention of using Times New Roman. The United States Supreme Court, however, dictates that all documents must be set in New Century Schoolbook. Both typefaces felt default, functional, and familiar. While they do not call attention to themselves at small size, they still command a sense of authority — attributes which the team hoped to emulate in their own design.

In reviewing historical source material, the team observed varying states of typographic degradation in the text of countless documents. As files were faxed, photocopied, and otherwise reproduced, the letterforms became bitmapped, bloated, warped, and were sometimes reduced to near-illegible forms. This particular aspect of variable legibility inspired subsequent experiments for future iterations of the fonts.

Times New Roman and New Century Schoolbook became the foundational pillars of legal typographic influence. The first goal was to draft something which simultaneously embodied both typefaces. While early tests of hybridization proved successful, the letterforms lacked a desired immediacy and contrast that could elevate them to both the abstract and conceptual, and ultimately be worthy of being incorporated into Kaphar and Betts's work.

An early point of inspiration was the Great Seal of the United States, which depicts an eagle grasping arrows in one talon and an olive branch in the other. This was embraced as a potent metaphor for the extremes in the legal system: cruelty

A pixel fits nicely into the joins on characters like H E, but required bending and shaping to be convincing on the n s.

Forest Young and Jeremy Mickel

and compassion, war and diplomacy, hard and soft, white and black. This logic was then applied to the letterforms: teardrop shapes became supple and round, while acute shapes became razor sharp. When this exaggerated contrast resulted in an amplified tension, the team knew they were on the right track.

Pushing ahead, the team looked back at the early bitmap studies and document references and wondered if they could synthesize those details into the the font. By incorporating negative shapes into the letterforms, the typeface could hint at the digital artifacts created through reproduction in fax machines and photocopiers.

Peter Saville's *Power, Corruption & Lies* album cover for New Order served as additional inspiration; the unassuming color bar on an otherwise mundane floral still life effortlessly merges contemporary and historical narratives. A pixel fits nicely into the joins on characters like *H* and *E*, but required bending and shaping to be convincing on the *n* and the *s*. Through trial and error, the letterform design followed an "inktrap logic"—to place negative shapes into as many of the glyphs as possible, with the additional pixel detail of a square tittle for the i dot and period.

It was always the hope to include bitmap grades of the font in order to reference the degradation of documents as they are reproduced through the legal process. As contemporary design moves through a zeitgeist of pixelation, with many incredible examples online, the team recalled the landmark designs by Susan Kare for the original Apple Operating System and many of Zuzana Licko's early digital fonts for the influential type foundry Emigre.

The team maintained a conceptual framework for the degraded versions; it's decidedly not merely an aesthetic. By providing a range of grades from subtly analog to nearly illegible, the typeface nods to the transformation and marginalization that many people face in the criminal justice system today, and specifically, the role and responsibility of the author of text to be conscious of legibility as a signature of power.

New Order, *Power, Corruption & Lies*, Factory Records, 1983 (Cover design: Peter Saville)

As part of the artists' dedication to social justice and legal equity, the Redaction fonts are distributed under the Open Font License at www.redaction.us. You can use them freely in your products and projects – print or digital, commercial or otherwise. However, you can't sell the fonts on their own. The fonts are available in 3 styles (regular, italic, bold) and 7 grades of degradation for a total of 21 fonts. All fonts have full character sets for Latin-1 language support.

Special thanks to Titus and Dwayne for extending the invitation to participate in this noble work. It is the team's hope that you will enjoy using the Redaction typeface.

Forest Young is currently the Global Head of Brand at Rivian, and previously served as the first Global Chief Creative Officer at Wolff Olins and as Senior Critic at the Yale University School of Art.

Jeremy Mickel is the founder of MCKL, a Los Angeles–based type foundry and design studio.

A range of grades from subtly analog to nearly illegible.

Redaction Typeface

List of Works

6: Titus Kaphar, *State #2 (Reginald Dwayne Betts)*, 2019. Oil, tar, and gold leaf on panel. 59 ½ × 75 ¾ × 2 ⅞ in.

7: Titus Kaphar, *The Fight for Remembrance I*, 2013. Oil on canvas. 62 × 50 in.

Archive 1

22: Titus Kaphar, *Shred Truth*, 2017. Oil on panel with nails. 59.5 × 51 in.

23: Reginald Dwayne Betts, "Crispus Attucks: For Natalie Diaz," 2022

24: Reginald Dwayne Betts, *Felon: Poems* (New York: W. W. Norton & Company, 2019); cover design: Sarahmay Wilkinson; cover art: Titus Kaphar, excerpt from *The Jerome Project*

25: Reginald Dwayne Betts, "Kites," 2022

26: Titus Kaphar, *Darker Than Cotton*, 2018. Oil on canvas. 63 × 36 in.

27: Reginald Dwayne Betts, "Benevolence," 2022

28: Reginald Dwayne Betts, "Volunteer Tomatoes," 2022

29: Titus Kaphar, *Unfit Description I*, 2014. Graphite on paper. 38 ³⁄₁₆ × 28 ¹¹⁄₁₆ × 1 ½ in. (framed)

30: Titus Kaphar, *New Enunciation*, 2021. Oil on canvas with mixed media. 71 ½ × 2 ¼ × 77 ¼ in.

31: Reginald Dwayne Betts, "Canary," 2022

32: Reginald Dwayne Betts, "Fugitive Slave Act of 1793 (redacted)," 2022

33: Titus Kaphar, *Nothing to See Here*, 2021. Oil on canvas with mixed media. 78 ¾ × 65 ¹⁵⁄₁₆ × 7 ⅞ inches.

34: Titus Kaphar, *Alternate Endings II*, 2016. Oil on canvas. 74 × 74 in.

35: Reginald Dwayne Betts, "Collective," 2022

36: Reginald Dwayne Betts, "Going Back," 2022

37: Titus Kaphar, *State #1 (Marcus Bullock)*, 2019. Oil, tar, and gold leaf on canvas. 75 ¾ × 59 ½ × 2 ¾ in.

Archive 2

86: Reginald Dwayne Betts, "Elephants in the Fall," 2022

87: Titus Kaphar, *Enough About You*, 2016. Oil on canvas with antique frame. 45 × 5 ½ × 70 in.

88: Titus Kaphar, *Ascension*, 2016. Oil on canvas with brass nails. 108 × 1 ½ × 84 in.

89: Reginald Dwayne Betts, "Memorial Hoops," 2022

90: Reginald Dwayne Betts, "White Peonies," 2022

91: Titus Kaphar, *Pushing Back the Light*, 2012. Oil and tar on canvas. 107 × 77 × 6 ½ in.

92: Titus Kaphar, *A Bitter Trade*, 2020. Oil on canvas. 60 × 48 in.

93: Reginald Dwayne Betts, "On Riots," 2022

94: Reginald Dwayne Betts, "Some Joy," 2022

95: Titus Kaphar, *Billy Lee: Portrait in Tar*, 2016. Oil and tar on canvas. 60 × 48 in.

96: Titus Kaphar, *Covered by Fear, Draped in Loss*, 2015. Oil on canvas. 60 × 48 in.

97: Reginald Dwayne Betts, "Birdsong," 2022

98: Reginald Dwayne Betts, "Essay on Reentry," 2022

99: Titus Kaphar, *Boys in Winter*, 2013. Oil on canvas. 64 × 64 × 1 ½ in.

Archive 3

140: Reginald Dwayne Betts, "Plumage," 2022

141: Titus Kaphar, *Monumental Inversions: George Washington*, 2016. Wood, blown glass, steel. 99 ¼ × 88 ¾ × 32 in.

142: Titus Kaphar, *Language of the Forgotten*, 2018. Charred white oak, high density urethane, glass, and LED lights. 7 ½ × 5 ½ × 4 ft.

143: Reginald Dwayne Betts, "Out back, daisies & crocuses," 2022

144: Reginald Dwayne Betts, "Morning," 2022

145: Titus Kaphar, *Forgotten Soldier*, 2019. Wood, glass, black pigment resin, LED lighting. 96 × 60 × 60 in.

146: Titus Kaphar, *Impressions of Liberty*, 2017. American sycamore, glass, high density urethane. 84 × 86 × 36 in.

147: Reginald Dwayne Betts, "Mercy," 2022

149: Reginald Dwayne Betts, "Ghazal," 2022

188: Reginald Dwayne Betts, "On the occasion of my 41st birthday: For Michael K. Williams," 2022

Acknowledgments

Redaction has always been more about what is present than what is absent. We've thanked our families, our wives, & our boys, both for the time that we've been away to do this work, & also believing that the work is meaningful. & we thank our mothers. These are the folks we can thank every day & it still wouldn't be enough. What we're called by them: husband, father, son – those are the things that have us dragging one foot after another on the toughest days. & we thank the folks that have suffered through incarceration, their families, the people who contributed their names to the civil suits that sparked this collaboration. You know, in deciding to stack images on top of each other to make etchings, it was to acknowledge that one of us is all of us, that we deserve the care of attention. & so, when you check these pages out, it's not so that you might discover the faces of folks in the cases, but for you to discover the face of your brother, your sister, your friends, to discover yourself – you see in this country, the ways that we incarcerate & forget becomes so much more possible because too many of us cannot imagine ourselves in those cells. But we know better. & we'd be remiss not to thank Elizabeth Alexander. Like us she is many things, & amongst those things a dear friend & New Haven, someone who knows that the heart of justice will always be art. Ain't enough to say about you & your influence on us. Dwayne keeps your book near his desk & a piece by Ficre on it. May we always walk through the doors that matter. Sarah Suzuki – you know we went to you to chop up ideas & walked away with a plan for an exhibit at MoMA PS1. The world deserves more people like you, who bring vision to every conversation. Titus says AC Hudgins first introduced him to Sarah, & so that means our thanks go to him as well. & of course, to Peter Eeley, who on those calls with Sarah believed that *Redaction* was going to be as important as we did. Thanks to Darren Walker, too, who has long known how art & justice are a part of the same story. & Aggie Gund who knows the importance of a book. & this team we've built. Natalie & Brianna are the glue, as capable at making the plans as they are at making sure the plans happen as our minds drift from possibility to possibility. & thanks to Forest Young. We should say that the beauty of all of this was how moments became plans, how tangents became centerpieces. Like the conversation at Fussy Coffee, where Titus was reminded of this time a classmate let him know how absurd it is to just choose any font – that classmate was Forest and that memory became connecting with Forest & Jeremy Mickel & that connection became the birth of the Redaction font. There is a print shop about two miles from Penn Station & Grand Central. & when we were searching for printers to work with, Erik Hougen stepped up. Him & Jeremy Ruiz weren't just the folks we worked at to bring these things to life – they were the cats we chopped it up with daily as we invented a vision. When Dwayne was talking about handmade paper, Erik was like you can't just use handmade paper to use handmade paper. Why don't you make it out of something that matters? & then, he introduced us to Ruth Lingen, & then we made paper out of the clothes of men that Dwayne has known for years, who were then doing life in prison. & we should mention them. & we can't forget Isaac Jaegerman, who was with us at Bowdoin College, where we first began imagining that this as possible. Isaac pushed us & guided us & had us digging in the shelves for random typeface & possibility. & James Goggin, who ran through seven thousand ideas with us on how to turn a book into the exhibit & poetry reading we wish all our folks could see. To Amanda Barrow for the assist. & to Amy Low & the reminder of how sometimes the writing matters, too, because it might remember joy. & to everyone who we've missed. To those who told us how absurd these ideas we've given breadth are. & to Christopher Tunstall, Rojai Fentress, Terrell Kelly, Anthony Winn, Markeese Turnage, Kevin Williams. When this started, they were all in prison. & most have found freedom. & we fight for those who still wait for mercy. Christopher, who we all called Juvie, died before he could see this work, just six months after he was released. & so, this is his memorial too, as it's the memorial for all the folks who ain't have a chance to become what they'd become, but who were enough, cause most of the time enough is all we got. *Redaction* ain't never been about us. It's always been about unmasking the need for freedom through art. & we thank you all.

Redaction

Copyright © 2023 by Titus Kaphar and Reginald Dwayne Betts

All rights reserved
Printed in the United States of America
First Edition

For information about permission to reproduce selections from this book, write to Permissions, W. W. Norton & Company, Inc., 500 Fifth Avenue, New York, NY 10110

For information about special discounts for bulk purchases, please contact W. W. Norton Special Sales at specialsales@wwnorton.com or 800-233-4830

Curators: Reginald Dwayne Betts and Titus Kaphar
Creative Direction: Forest Young
Curatorial Assistants:
Natalie Renee, Brianna Walker
Design Direction & Book Production:
James Goggin, Practise
Design Assistant: Amanda Barrow
Color Separations: Sebastiaan Hanekroot and Rossella Castello, Colour & Books

Type: Redaction (Jeremy Mickel and Forest Young, 2019)
Paper: Fedrigoni Sirio Color Black 170 gsm, Fedrigoni Golden Star K Extra White 160 gsm, Sappi Magno Volume 135 gsm
Print: die Keure, Bruges, Belgium

ISBN 978-1-324-00682-4

W. W. Norton & Company, Inc.,
500 Fifth Avenue, New York, NY 10110
www.wwnorton.com

W. W. Norton & Company Ltd.,
15 Carlisle Street, London W1D 3BS

1 2 3 4 5 6 7 8 9 0

Image Credits
6: Photo by Kris Graves; 10–11: Photo by Rob McKeever; 12–13: Photo by Matthew Septimus; 30: Photo by Rob McKeever; 33: Photo by Rob McKeever; 37: Photo by Kris Graves; 38–39: Photo by Rob McKeever; 43–49: Photos by Omar Hamati; 92: Photo by Christopher Gardner; 95: Photo by Jeremy Lawson; 193 (top right): New Order cover courtesy of Peter Saville Studio.